FREEDOM IS…

A BOOK/JOURNAL WITH A TWIST

KATHLEEN L. WENSEL

Trafford
PUBLISHING

Order this book online at www.trafford.com/07-0973 or email orders@trafford.com
Most Trafford titles are also available at major online book retailers.

© Copyright 2008 Kathleen L. Wensel.
Edited by Barbara Ardinger
Kathleen L. Wensel, Front Cover, Media, PA
Donna Billingsley – Photography, Back Cover, Media, PA
William McNitt, Archivist, Gerald R. Ford Presidential Library and Museum,
Ann Arbor, MI 48109

Note for Librarians: A cataloguing record for this book is available from Library and Archives
Canada at www.collectionscanada.ca/amicus/index-e.html

Printed in Victoria, BC, Canada.

ISBN: 978-1-4251-2812-8

*We at Trafford believe that it is the responsibility of us all, as both individuals and corporations,
to make choices that are environmentally and socially sound. You, in turn, are supporting this
responsible conduct each time you purchase a Trafford book, or make use of our publishing services.
To find out how you are helping, please visit www.trafford.com/responsiblepublishing.html*

*Our mission is to efficiently provide the world's finest, most comprehensive book publishing
service, enabling every author to experience success. To find out how to publish your book, your
way, and have it available worldwide, visit us online at www.trafford.com/10510*

www.trafford.com

North America & international
toll-free: 1 888 232 4444 (USA & Canada)
phone: 250 383 6864 ♦ fax: 250 383 6804
email: info@trafford.com

The United Kingdom & Europe
phone: +44 (0)1865 722 113 ♦ local rate: 0845 230 9601
facsimile: +44 (0)1865 722 868 ♦ email: info.uk@trafford.com

10 9 8 7 6 5

DEDICATIONS
This book is dedicated to:

George P. Wensel Sr. & Lillian Werner Wensel (grandparents); William T. Garvey & Delia Creighton Garvey (grandparents); George P. Wensel Jr. & Mary T. Garvey Wensel (parents); George P. Wensel III, (brother); Dr. Timothy J. Ryan, (cousin); Edward T. Doyle (uncle Ducky); Howard Wensel (uncle Cy), Russell Faith (Composer); Sister Marie Antonio, High School Spanish Teacher. They now live with God in Heaven!

Karen C. Creely (daughter) and Edward J. Creely, Jr. (son); Brian C. Wensel & Emily Kittler Wensel, (brother and sister-in-law); Brent and Colin Wensel; Sha Odell; Rosalyn Benjet; Darryl and Ruby Austin; Becky Chambers (Hairdresser); Father Joseph McLaughlin, Headmaster, Archmere Academy; B.J.P. Ladson; Suzi Myer, Troy Laws; Layton Smith (Accountant); Kenneth West (Attorney); Jaime Atkinson; Ron Williams; Harris & Andrea Fellman; Christian Stettler; Ken and Emerald Aagaard; Donald Trump; Bill & Melinda Gates; Oprah Winfrey; and Professor Martin E. Goldstein (Widener University) who was so excited for me when I told him about the book. Professor Goldstein is a wonderful teacher.

To all my friends at Acme Markets (part of Supervalu Stores): Frank McElroy (Store Manager) Chris Merchanti and John Gallagher

(Assistant Store Managers),Marty Albert, Jason Anszis, Ty Asbury, Kara Bacchia, Brendan Barnett, James Barrett, Barb Bechtel, Emilio Bonilla, Stephanie Borriello, John Burke, Loretta Burke, Stacey Busch, Jenifer Capuano, Tim Cody, Deborah Costello, Jim Curtis, Kathy D'aiterio, Christine Donohue, Larry Dunn, Frank Falvey, John Fittipaldi, Ashley Fortune, Ryan Fortune, David Green, Amy Herkness, Frank Higgins, Darlene Jackson, Melonie Kaczynski, Joe Kerr, Min Jung Kim, John Koch, Susanna Lange, Carol Maturo, Karen Moletteri, John Moletteri, Harry Moore, Michael Nepa, Stanley Nowaczyk, Mark Oberg, Glenn Parsons, Steve Quagliarello, Jaime Quinlan, Mary Sciallo, Mike Sizemore, Cynthia Smitherman, Bill Tate, Brenda Turchi, Lisa Tursi, Maryann Ward, Ellen Wienckowski, Jesse Wienckowski, Amelia Wilber, Robert Wood, Mike Yeager.

> Judy Spires – President – Acme Markets
> Andrew Gillian – Acme Markets – Granite Run
> Darlene Wetten – Bakery Manager – Acme Markets – Ridley
> Judy Kerr – Assistant Manager – Devon
> Andrew Randall – College Student
> Sherry Schievert - Granite Run
> Tom Clarke - Acme Markets - Granite Run
> Toni Kaczynski – Acme Markets – Granite Run
> John Koch – Acme Markets – Naamans Rd
> To all the people at the Supervalu chain of stores across the country.
> Thanks to all the staff at the Media Inn, Media, PA. When in Delaware Country, PA, stay at the Media Inn.

All of these people listed above have had a profound impact on my life.

To all the people who knew I could achieve my dreams and hung in there with me. Love you all always! Thank you, all!

To all the people who have dreams —live your dreams to the fullest. Stay focused, no matter what. Be persistent, have tenacity, and a zest for life. Almost everything is negotiable. There is always a way. As Sir Winston Churchill said "Never, never, never, never give up." (One of the shortest speeches, but one of the best!)

To all the people who died on September 11, 2001 in New York, Virginia, and Pennsylvania, and all their wives, children, husbands, parents, aunts, uncles, grandparents, brothers, sisters, cousins and friends left behind by this act of cruelty. Know that they are with you always; and we will carry them in our hearts, forever!

To all the Freedom-Loving People around the World! This includes all the people who want to be free. They walk with freedom in their hearts! Freedom to live your life is what it is all about!

REMEMBER.
FREEDOM IS…

LIFE
IS NOT
A
DRESS REHERSAL
IT IS
THE
MAIN EVENT!

There is a wonderful reason for…

FREEDOM IS…

A BOOK/JOURNAL WITH A TWIST.

HOW THIS BOOK/JOURNAL BEGAN

On August 1, 2001, I awoke very sick, all over, not knowing why. When I stood up I was very dizzy, and I had a headache, a stomachache, a heartache, the worst feeling of dread and a thousand pounds on each of my shoulders. That day, I thought I was going to die, but I could not figure out why. What's going on? I asked myself. I am a very positive person, but what I was feeling on this day was something much different. I felt fine the night before, but now my mind was racing. I was thinking, *I must write down my thoughts,* so I sat down and started writing. Even with what was going on with me and how bad I was feeling, I had to write my thoughts. My brain would not turn off until I went to sleep. It was up and ready to go, day after day. My body was saying, *Stay in bed till all this passes,* but I was in the middle of a conflict between my brain and my body, not where I wanted to be.

Since I am a positive person, I kept going. (Being Taurus the Bull can be good at times). Why was I writing? These words are what I've always believed. But why was I writing them now?

I believe that there is a reason for everything. I kept writing. I remembered what Sir Winston Churchill said, *"If you are going through hell, keep going."* So I kept going. *What's up with this?* I wondered. *Look what's going on around me.* Going through something horrible and at the same time joyful; how could this happen? But it was happening. Something horrendous was going to happen, but I did not know what. My gut reaction works most of the time. I had all the questions and no answers.

Each day the feelings of dread, heartache, thinking I am going to die, got stronger and stronger, even though, I was having fun writing my thoughts. My feelings on a daily basis were going up and down. That was odd because I am usually very happy most of the time. I did not understand how that could be happening, and I did not know why. Something was terribly wrong. (I felt like I was going to throw up. I only throw up every ten years.) Who would I tell? What would I say, and how could I explain *anything* I was going through to anyone? I did not know what was going on. Who would listen to me?

No medicine could help what I was going through. I decided to stay calm and play this out to the end. I figured I would keep the faith, keep focused, and keep writing. This went on day after day. The feelings of dread, heartache, stomachache, horrific headaches were a thousand times worse each day. Not knowing what to do, I just kept writing. *Questions? Who has control of my thoughts?* (A higher power, God) *Where am I going with this? What is causing this awful dread? Why was I given this project? When am I going to know the answer? How can I explain this to anyone? Whatever is going to happen, the world will see it, and the world will change, forever.*

Again, I had all the questions, but no answers.

Just stay focused, I kept telling myself, and keep thinking thoughts *and jotting down my thoughts. Keep writing. Now, I am going to take this to a higher level. From a book to a book/journal.* (I have written my thoughts, now you can write your thoughts about Freedom).

Then the phone rang. I flipped on the TV. The *Who? What? Where? When? Why?* and *How?* were right in front of me. My questions were beginning to have answers. As the first Twin Tower fell, then the second Twin Tower fell, then the Pentagon was hit, then the plane hit the field in Shankesville, Pennsylvania.

As I watched the plane hit the Second Tower, my question was,

Who did this to us? My thoughts said, *Terrorists.* Who else? The garage under the World Trade Center was bombed in 1993. They couldn't level the buildings from the bottom, so they used our airplanes and leveled both of them from the top. Where are the other terrorists? How many more planes will be driven into other buildings? Are they in the air or are more on the ground? What caused this action? When did we know or not know about this action? Why did this happen? How is the United States going to handle what happened today? The terrorists used our own planes to hit us and killed all the people on the planes and many of the people in the Twin Towers, plus some people in the Pentagon. It was just incredible. How could this happen? Seems to me someone was not watching the friendly skies or anything else.

I realized that I lived through a future nightmare. As I watched the second plane hit the Second Tower, all the dread, fear, heartache, headache, a thousand pounds on each of my shoulders...all these left my body at the same time. I felt a million pounds lighter. I was back to my normal feelings. Realizing that what I had felt for forty-one days prior to September 11, 2001, was what millions of people worldwide were now feeling, I had to sit down. Knowing that something bad was going to happen tells me that my gut reaction is alive and well and living in America.

I was not surprised that a tragedy of this magnitude took place on September 11, 2001. As the days passed, the feelings were stronger and more intense. Whatever was going to happen was going to happen at sometime and September 11, 2001, happened to be the day. (I really do not want to have those feelings, again). I hope someone (God) is listening upstairs to me downstairs.

The other reason this book/journal was written is if I ever wake up with the same feelings again, I will know what to do (stay calm and focused) and who to call (the police, the White House, the Pentagon, Homeland Security, my senators, and members of Congress.

Through all the forty-one days of darkness, I saw a positive light. Why do this *FREEDOM IS*...a Book/Journal with a Twist, now?

Why not, now? The book part is my thoughts and words. The journal part is your thoughts and words. Together, they become a book/journal treasure to keep and pass on from generation to generations to come.

FREEDOM IS…is an easy, special, fun book/journal for all people who love freedom and future people who will love their new freedom to enjoy at any age. Whether they live in America or around the world, freedom-loving people will read my freedoms, think about their freedoms, and write their own freedoms and future freedoms in the journal part of the book. Everyone is an individual. Everyone likes different freedoms. All freedom-loving people make their own choices.

FREEDOM IS…being free.

What is Freedom? According to the Oxford English Dictionary. Noun.

1. the power or right to act, speak or think freely.
2. the state of being free.
3. (freedom from) exemption or immunity from.
4. unrestricted use of something (dog has the run of the house)
5. a special privilege or right of access, especially that of full citizenship of a particular city given to a public figure as an human.

Chapters

THERE ARE ALL TYPES OF FREEDOMS IN OUR LIVES...

All my freedoms are connected because they are my freedoms and they are how I live my life. All that people do are connected to different types of freedoms in their lives.

1

FREEDOM IS...
The United States Of America

I would like to thank the Founding Fathers for putting the Declaration of Independence together in 1776. I would like to give each of them a hug (I give lots of hugs, people need them), it was not easy 232 years ago, starting a new country. They did a great job. Suppression was no longer an option. Freedom was.

Today, we are still working on it, but like then, it is not easy with all the terrorist threats, the oil crisis, the economy, hurricanes, strange weather, global warming and just plain crazy things going on around the planet. We are not a perfect country, (no country is), but we continue to work on it. That is what we do. Everyone on the planet is not going to like us, we understand that, but we still help and will continue to do so.

2

FREEDOM IS...
Be Fearless

Before you can take a stand with anyone else you have to take a stand with yourself. What do I want to do? What is my passion? Always keep records of my thoughts and what I am doing now, tomorrow and in the future. Make lists for today and tomorrow. (My lists are short) Try to get all the tasks done. If you do not get the whole list done, do not beat yourself up about it. If not, add the tasks not completed to the top of tomorrows lists. It really works. It's fun.

I have adopted *"Fearless"* as my middle name. There were times in my life that were full of fear, my marriage was a threat to my life. Until I spoke out I lived in fear. Speak out it will make you *"Fearless"* too.

Speaking your mind is a good thing. I like people who are straight-forward. I can deal with straight-forward talk, because you know where you stand. Being wishy-washy does not work for me.

3

FREEDOM IS...
Be Kind To Yourself

Beating yourself up over mistakes of the past is a mistake. You cannot change the past. One of my quotes is, "There is no future in the past." We can learn from the past, but do not live there."

We all make mistakes. Just move on into your future. Knowing who you are at this time is the key. Make your life what you want it to be. Take your time. Think. Control what you can and do not concern yourself with anything else.

4

FREEDOM IS...
Believe In Yourself

Before you can believe in anything else you have to believe in yourself. This is the key to what you want in your life. I have achieved many things in my life and if I did not believe I could do it, I probably would not have been able to do many things in my life.

From real estate, travel, retail and wholesale marketing and sales, radio show guest across America, commercials, telemarketing, seminar speaker, model and teacher, entrepreneur and now author. In the works are websites, a radio show, TV appearances, ebooks with more to come.

Just keep going is the best thing to do for yourself. Whatever I believe, I can achieve. Whatever you believe, you can achieve. Just close your eyes and you can see your future. It's that simple!

Do not let family, friends, associates, co-workers, etc. tell you what to do. People get jealous when they think you are going to be in a better position than they are right now. If a person is really happy for you, they will tell you that you can do it and they are happy for you.

Example: Lottery winners: Family and friends will get really ticked off if they are not given any money from the winnings. They didn't win the pie, but they expect a piece of the pie. What's up with that? If the winner of the lottery wants to help on a one time basis, that's up to the winner. Some people want a monthly handout. If not, then they will not speak to the winner again. Maybe that's a good thing for the winner of the lottery.

5

FREEDOM IS…
Change

This is good for me. When I do something for a long time it gets real old, real fast. People I know feel the same way. Change is special and people should be willing to change when change is about to happen. Some changes are good, some bad, change happens whether we want it to happen or not happen. Different circumstances in our lives bring lots of changes in our lives.

Whether a person is a mogul or a stay-at-home, change happens. (Some stay-at-homes are Internet Millionaires.) Sometimes there is one change or many changes in our lives. A move, a job change, a new love, a divorce, a new baby, a new hair-do and hair color, whatever it is, accept it. Change is good.

I was always ready for a change. Change is a new beginning, a new start for different parts of my life. I am a Taurus and as a Taurus one characteristic of a Taurus is that we do not like change. In this case, I am a Taurus that does like change. How cool is that for me? Change is good. I just changed my hair color.

I know there are some people who do not want to change. Everyone makes their own choices.

6

FREEDOM IS...
Claim Your Freedoms

Put together what you want to do for yourself. I see so many unhappy people. I see them all the time. There is so much going on in their lives. Life is so complicated for them. Their lives are chaotic. This is not good for their families, their health, and their lives.

People have told me that they do not want "to do this" anymore, meaning that they do not want to be married anymore. They do not like their job anymore. This keys into change. They need changes in their lives. The more they think and talk about not liking different things in their lives, the more they need to change. Changes in their lives are going to happen sooner or later. Sooner is better!

My life has been quite a ride so far and I am looking forward to continuing the ride into the future. Throughout the years, we must take care of ourselves, first. When women are happy life is good, if not, look out! Taking care of ourselves gives us freedom. Taking care of our freedoms should be foremost in everyone's lives.

Get rid of whatever isn't working for you. Don't wait as long as I did. (married twenty-nine years) Life is too short for anything else. It's just that simple!

Think you're free while living in fear? Think yourself free, soon you will be free. Freedom takes the fear away. People ask me why am I always happy? And I answer, "Because, I am free."

7

―――――――――――――――――

FREEDOM IS...
Common Sense

This is so crucial nowadays. This is for every day of the year. Everyone is so busy and time is of the essence throughout the year, especially during the holidays. Ladies, watch your pocketbooks. (I see pocketbooks left in the seat of the supermarket carts.) Carry you pocketbook with you, at all times. The crooks are waiting for you to put it down. If, you do, they can steal your identity. This is not cool for you.

Gentlemen, watch your wallets everyday of the year. Gentlemen, keep your wallets in your front pocket, not your back pocket. Remember, crooks are waiting and watching, when you least expect it.

Ladies and gentlemen watch your children. (Children left alone sitting in the seats of the carts at the supermarket with no parental supervision around them.) If you have lots of packages, take them home and then come back to do more shopping. The crooks are just waiting for you to put all the goodies in the car or van. Then the crooks will take them home for their family and friends. This goes for all the year, not just the holidays.

Watch if someone is hanging around you at the mall or anywhere else. If so, tell the salesperson, and they will call security. If something does not feel right, safeguard yourself first. (Put yourself first.

Do not shrug off the feelings of impending doom in your life.) If you are in a parking lot and feel that someone is following you, use your cell phone to call the police. Then go into a store and tell the manager what is going on. Stay in the store until the police come. Protect yourself at all times. Travel in pairs, not alone. Do not walk late at night unless you have a group with you, male or female.

Be aware of what is around you at all times. Learning to be aware is not difficult. It is fun. Let your gut reaction come alive and see what happens. Your gut reaction will keep you safe and the people around you safe. More help—take a self-defense class (judo, kick-boxing).

Nowadays, we have to look around for strange things that we see. Anything that looks strange in your neighborhood probably does not belong there. Just call the police, FBI. Homeland Security, they will handle it.

8

FREEDOM IS…
Conscience

Individual thoughts, what a beautiful thing. I was not one to follow the crowd. Getting in trouble (drinking, smoking, drugs) was not on my agenda. Drinking, smoking and drugs, cause more problems in the family, at work, and in life.

My conscience is my friend who keeps me straight. Either right or wrong is the answer. Positive or negative, no middle ground. I have found that most people know right from wrong. If people did not know right from wrong, why would they run when the police come? My conscience is there to keep me straight. Yes, sometimes it might really feel good to go the negative way and really get back at someone who caused me a problem. That's only human nature. Don't do it! Whatever you have to do, do it legally and karma will also step into the picture. Stay on the right track and giving back will be easy. Everyone that has ever tried to hurt me has been hit by God and karma coming back around at them. It's really something how God and karma works.

When you drink and drive, an innocent person or persons can be hurt or killed. My daughter and her friend we almost killed by a drunk driver and they were pronounced dead at the scene. When my daughter and her friend hit the lights at the hospital door, they both woke up. Happily, they both survived. They got a second chance at life. I call it a miracle. Thank you, God.

Eventually, sobering up happens and a person would have to look in the mirror and see himself or herself for what they really are. They are hazardous to themselves and everyone around them. Reality is looking at them in the mirror. Sometimes drunks will get a clue and choose to sober up for themselves and their families. Going to weekly meetings and getting their lives back on the right track is the key for a better life and maybe a longer and happier life.

Sometimes drunks don't want to change. They would rather drink, not face the reality of their deeds. When a drunk does not take responsibility for his or her actions, they are in denial that they have a problem. This creates a real problem because they think they are not doing anything wrong. They think what they are doing is normal. Reality may or may not set in for them, until they finally kill themselves or an innocent person or family, when they are behind the wheel drunk. I guess going to jail for some drunk drivers is the only way that they will finally get it. When they finally go to jail and sobriety sets in big time, I imagine, that is the final reality check point.

Smoking. I tried it once when I was a teenager. I turned green, and decided never to smoke again. I always remembered the picture hanging on the wall, in grade school. It showed two lungs. One was a healthy lung (nice and pink), the other, a black lung (damaged beyond repair.) I choose to live healthy.

Drugs. What's the point of frying your brain? This never made any sense to me to harm my brain. Sometimes life can be trying enough. Why add to it? Why end up with half a brain by doing drugs?

My best example of why I do not do any of these things: I was born at seven months and weighed 2 pounds 14 ounces. I was in the hospital from May to September, when I went home in September I weighed five pounds.

I have always had a good relationship with God. I've made my share of mistakes, but they are my mistakes. I have learned from them and I moved on.

The doctors gave me no chance to live and only 50 percent chance for my mother. Mom went blind, had convulsions, her kidneys locked. She had eclampsia. We both survived. Mom lived till June 13, 1987 and I was given a chance at life, so why would I want to blow it by drinking, smoking and doing drugs.

9

FREEDOM IS...
Courage

Everyone has some type of courage, hidden or out front. People are put in different situations (I call them tests) to see how they can handle them. I have been through a lot of different circumstances in my life. Real life is a game. Learn how to play it, what to do and don't do, and have fun.

Mistakes. I am the first one to admit it when I am wrong. The one big mistake I made was marrying the wrong person. I paid for that one for twenty-nine years. People, listen to your mothers and fathers. The only time I did not listen to my mother and my friend Rosalyn, I made the biggest mistake of my life by marrying the wrong person. I had the right children, but married the wrong man. But, I had the courage to divorce him. I fired my attorney, did my own paper work, and I love my freedom.

Have the courage to take a risk. Whether starting a business, moving, breaking up, taking a stand, stopping a bully/harasser, looking for a new job, making money online...whatever, make sure it's legal, then just do it. You will never know what will happen until you do it. Yes, it will go one way or the other. Either way, just keep going. Taking a risk for the positive does not mean that you do anything stupid and crazy.

Do not listen to the detractors of your dreams. That includes family, friends, neighbors, co-workers. Stay focused and follow your dreams. Make everyday a day closer to your dreams becoming a reality. You will be so glad that you listened to yourself.

I think the words, "What might have been" are sad words because they mean, you will never know. (Take "what might have been" out of your vocabulary.) You will never know if you do not try. When you try and it doesn't work the way you want it to, keep going. Try again and do not give up. When you give up, you are lost and things will not change until you change them. Remember what Winston Churchill, said: "When you are going through hell, keep going" and "Never, never, never, never give up."

John F. Kennedy wrote, "*Profiles in Courage.*" Everyone should read this book. It shows different types of courage by different people throughout the years.

The movie "Bucket List" with Jack Nicolson and Morgan Freeman. Everyone should have a "Bucket List" Write down what you really want to do before your return to Heaven. Whether it is sky-diving, Nascar racing, walking the Great Wall of China, climbing Mount Everest, walking across the United States for a great cause. Whatever it is, start making your list and do what is on the list. It really is your heart's desire. Think about it, sit down and start writing.

10

FREEDOM IS…
Creativity

Without creativity, what would we see in the universe? Look at what we have: The Empire State Building, The Taj Mahal, The Palace of Versailles, The Sydney Opera House, The Las Vegas Strip, Sports Stadiums (Citizens Bank Park, Philadelphia, PA; Fenway Park, Boston, MA) Beautiful golf courses: (Pebble Beach, CA), PGA courses, Museums: the Guggenheim, NYC, the Getty Museum in Malibu, CA, Cities, states and countries: Las Vegas, New York City, the State of Florida, the State of Colorado, Cape Cod. Rincon, Puerto Rico; Vancouver, British Columbia; The Pacific Coast Highway, CA; Pepperdine University, overlooking the Pacific Ocean in Malibu, CA; Victorian Cape May, New Jersey. Notre Dame University, South Bend, IN, The Christ of the Andes, Rio. Milwaukee, WI. Chicago, IL. Disney World, Orlando, FL. Central Park, NYC. The Great Wall of China. Music: waltzes, rock and roll, motown, country. Monaco. The Golden Gate Bridge. Venice, Italy (built on water). Ireland, Spain, Switzerland. Australia. Figi. France. Great Britian. Greece. Fashions worldwide. The Internet. Houses, communities, buildings, furnishing. Movies & TV shows, Broadway Shows, Cars. The Planet is a beautiful place. Everything that we see was created by some very special person.

God the first creator, created the universe. Creative people took the Earth that was created by God and made it more beautiful. Their creative ability made it a beautiful place for all of us to travel to great places and live our lives in different places.

11

FREEDOM IS...
Decisions
(Good–Bad–Indifferent)

Making a decision is a part of life. The kinds of decisions that we make, do make a difference in our lives. I know sometimes it is very hard to make, what is considered, the right decision. Make the best decisions for yourself. You know what is good for you, no one else really does.

Some decisions happen quickly. (Like getting negative people out of your life) Some decisions are made, but happen at a later time. (Such as: a job and/or a move). Some decisions when made may take years, but changes will happen. (To end my marriage)

For myself: when I make a decision it is a done deal. When I say I'm done. I mean I am done. (People that really know me, know this to be true) Most Entrepreneurs make quick decisions and stick to them. It has always been easy for me to make a decision. Having to make a decision on the spot is easy. Learn to do it.

Do not take a long time to make a decision. The longer you take to make a decision, the more confused you will get. You are going to have to make a decision one way or the other, so make it sooner than later.

12

FREEDOM IS…
Defended

We have been a country for 232 years. We have certainly had our ups and downs. Protecting our freedom is every Americans right any infringement is against our independence.

In your own neighborhood, watch out for things that look strange, like something does not belong there (any strange paper bags, backpacks, cases, anything left alone). Stay away from it and call the police, the FBI and Homeland Security. Check in your cities and towns to see if there is a citizen group that works along with the police. You will learn from them what to do and how to handle different situations in your community.

Look out for your neighbors. We are not living here alone. It only takes one person to stop a tragedy from happening. The police and the feds will handle it. Just call them. The lives your save may include yours and the ones you love. We were hit a few times and I am sure that we will be hit, again. Maybe next time we will be better prepared.

What do the terrorists want? They want to kill us. Kidnappers just want money. Terrorists just want to kill us. They may not like the freedom we have. It may be very threatening to the terrorists. The terrorists like to be in control and they want us to leave their land and go home. We can keep our freedoms by defending our freedoms and our homeland.

13

FREEDOM IS...
Democracy

The freedom to vote for or not vote for who is running for state or federal office. Our choice. People do not always like the people who are running. Sometimes the personality, looks, platform, messages, body language and political commercials are just a turnoff to the voting public. Instead of tearing each other apart, just say what they are going to do to help all the people of the United States, not just a chosen few.

Americans want to hear the truth. Maybe, some politicians think we (the American People) do not like to hear the truth, but that's not true. The truth is better because, sooner or later, the truth will rear its head and bite whomever on the butt. Truth in the beginning is better. Americans can forgive, but not forget, and then we move on. When the lies keep coming, it is very hard to take, because it is what it is. A lie is a lie is a lie. Body language speaks volumes. It's amazing how that works.

All the negative politicking turns off the public. Maybe the public already has enough negativity in their lives (marriage, work, sickness, war) and they do not need to see the politicians in this country acting like little kids, or worse than little kids. Negativity was running wild and at its worse in the 2006 elections. It was painful to watch and listen to. What is the point of politicians going after each other? Why all the fighting? What's up with the red and blues states? I thought we were all Americans. When you play nice, it will benefit you more in life.

Everything has a way of catching up, one way or another. There is so much stuff that people have forgotten about in their lives that ends up on the Internet. (One picture is always worth a thousand words.) The candidates should only run a positive campaigns and say what they are going to do for all the American people, not just a chosen few.

The American people have spoken loud and clear. Everyone in the political arena in Washington, DC, and other cities in this country, should take notice. The people changed the political landscape once. They can do it again and again. Learn to work together. After all, whether we are Republican or Democrat or Independent, the voters are all Americans, all living in the United States of America and around the world.

Instead of having months and months and months of politicking before the election, we should change it to only six months. That would stop all the name calling and get straight to the point of what the politicians are going to do for all the American people.

14

FREEDOM IS…
Economic

Owning our own homes, our businesses, getting rid of individual debt. Save as much as you can, start your own business at home. Looking for a better job, or more money, sometimes you may have to relocate to get what they want. Moving can be fun. Make it fun. Want a better job? Have a hobby? Go to the internet. Learn how to put your website together from A to Z. Put this together while you are working your day job. Then, when it takes off for four to six months, only then can you quit. This will get you where you want to be. Then you can let go of your job working for someone else. Now you can be your own boss. I am doing this for myself.

Remember, set your own pay rate for yourself. Do not let anyone else set it for you. When you work for yourself you are in charge of what you make each week. Think Big!

I want to have more freedom which will give me more time to help others and to give back to the communities across the country and around the world. Starting by giving back to The Leary Firefighters Foundation.

Go where the jobs are. Go where it is inexpensive to live. The states west of Pennsylvania to the California border and south of Washington DC are less expensive to live in. California and from

Washington, DC to Boston are more expensive to live in. Check out all the prospects. You may love what you see. If you have to move, just do it. It will probably be the best thing you can do for yourself. Check the area from A to Z. Furniture from the Northeast will not go with Florida or southwest of the U.S. (Nevada, New Mexico, Arizona and Texas)

Sell what you can. You do not want to have a big moving bill. If you have not used it or worn it for a year, sell it, give it away or throw it away. If in doubt throw it out. You will never know if you don't move. You will always wonder, *what if?* Get rid of the *what ifs* in your life. *What ifs* will stress you out. You will not be happy. You will never live your dreams.

15

FREEDOM IS...
Education...Discipline

It is a triangle: teachers, students, parents working together. This is the key to success.

Learning entails discipline (at home and school), not disruption. Parents are the parents, not the child's best friend. Disciplining children (without beating them) is not a bad thing. Learning *yes or no* is the key. Disruption takes away the freedom to learn from the students who want to learn. I have found over the years that children like boundaries. How else are they going to learn? Boundaries learned early give them freedom later in life. Good rules for life make excellent citizens. I have always found that being disciplined will give you lots of freedom in your life.

Talking to each other is the key. There are some very scary things going on in the grammar schools, middle schools, high schools, colleges and universities. Students, to prevent a tragedy talk to your parents and your teachers. (Parents were once students themselves, maybe some still are going to school) There is nothing that you say to your parents that they have not heard or seen before.

Be part of the solution, not part of the problem. Communication is the key.

Children are our future. Kids are not dumb or stupid. They actually know what is going on in the world. Much of the world is at their fingertips nowadays. Cable is worldwide: they can see wars, earthquakes, tsunamis. Computers, iPods, Blackberries, iPhone. Everything is a click away on the computer and television.

FREEDOM IS...
Endangered

When freedom is in danger of being taken away or has already been taken away by tyrants (tyrants are the only ones with the freedom, everyone does what the tyrant says to do) people are in danger. Freedom is lost.

I believe everyone should be free to live their lives. If they are not, then they are not free. This does not include criminals.

All it takes is one tyrant in each country, and fear sets in. The people are afraid to do anything for fear of retaliation. Freedom will take longer to achieve. Eventually, things will change for the better.

17

FREEDOM IS…
Equality…Respect

Most people are decent people. At the present time, I am a happy cashier at Acme Markets and I treat everyone of my customers with respect. I do not care what a person's skin color is white, red, black, yellow, brown, sky blue pink—it doesn't matter to me.

People have a lot going on in their lives. Some people bring their stuff (anger) with them when they go food shopping. (They shouldn't, but they do.) I usually have them laughing by the time they leave my line. If a person is decent, I will deal with them. If not, I call security.

We are all citizens on this planet. Getting along means survival for all of us. Putting our talents together for mankind should be in the forefront for all of us on the planet. Discover what your true talent is. What do you really like to do? Do you have a hobby, play an instrument, invent something? Whatever it is, start to think about it. It is part of you. Do not be afraid to bring it out. You will be surprised at what will happen positively in your life.

Get out of the box. Learn to relax. You will have fun and love your new life.

Fighting, killing, bombing….who wins? No one. A lot of people get killed or manned for life. What's the point? No one is taking anything with them when they go home to Heaven, Purgatory or Hell. People may be able to buy everything else and pay off a lot of people on Earth, but they should not try it at the Pearly Gates. You cannot pay cash, checks, money orders, debit or credit cards, stocks, bonds, real estate or buy anyone off to get through the Pearly Gates. That's not going to happen. There is a Final Reality Check at the Pearly Gates.

I bet it is a real shocker for some people when they do not get through the Pearly Gates and are escorted in the other direction. (I would like to be sitting on a cloud watching this senario. I would probably fall off laughing to hear all the *but I's* and *they did it, not me.*) Some of the Final Judgments must be a comedy routine. God must laugh. Talk about Reality in their face. Case closed!

It's not what you have in your wallet that gets you into heaven. What gets you into heaven is all the good deeds that you do for others, how you help people, not hurt people. This is what gets you into heaven. God doesn't like ugly! Good deeds in the book of life (everyone has a life book in the big library in the sky) at the Pearly Gates gets people into Heaven. Remember, *the Final Justice Belongs to God.*

18

FREEDOM IS…
Faith, Hope, Love

America is built on faith, hope and love of freedom. Our ancestors came from far and wide to enjoy what America offers to its citizens and future citizens. It took a lot of guts, along with faith, hope and love to leave their homelands and come to a strange land. But they did it. They did not know many people here or maybe no one at all, but they came anyway!

People came because they had to come. It was part of their lives, something they had to do. Their spirits soared higher than the sky. It was a new adventure they were going on.

Many people never saw their homelands or family's again, but they came, anyway. And people are still adventurous and still coming to America. It's somewhat like moving from one part of this country to another part (but on a smaller scale because we are in the same country). Leaving family and friends and moving to a new city, not knowing anyone there, may be daunting but exciting. Our ancestors did not have the communications that we have now. In the 20th and 21st centuries, we have iPods, cell phones, computers, and the abundance of travel to return to their homelands for visits.

I love this country. With all its faults and triumphs, it is young and still learning.

Without freedom, nothing can be accomplished.

19

FREEDOM IS...
Forever

Without freedom, I could not do what I am doing. Since I got a divorce, I really realized this to be true for me. I cannot speak for everyone, but it is true for me. Total freedom for me is working for myself. I have one more step to go to leave my cashier job and be totally free by working for myself. I am on my way to doing this. This book, websites, joint ventures, coaching, seminars, teleseminars, a radio show, giving back to The Leary Firefighters Foundation gives me a worldwide audience.

Being a citizen of the world is another thing that is great. Helping people gives me a sense of self. Seeing a smile on someone's face is such a pleasant feeling. Making someone smile and seeing their eyes light up is something really special. I believe most people are basically the same.

Some of the proceeds from this book will benefit The Leary Firefights Foundation (I love firefighter's). Giving back to the community, I will help people live their dreams. They can follow what I did, and then they can show others what to do. It will mushroom across this country, and around the world, over and over, again.

20

FREEDOM IS…
Forgiveness

When we forgive the people who have hurt us, we heal our hearts and our souls and our spirits. It is the best thing to do for ourselves.

Have you every seen people hold a grudge? Some people hold grudge's for a year, five years, ten years, fifteen years, twenty years or a lifetime and any amount in between. Why? What is the point?

The people who are holding the grudge's usually have health problems. (Guess what caused the health problems?) Most of the time, the people who the grudge is against do not care, they are living their lives.

There are things that happen in life that are sometimes out of our control. Sometimes good, sometimes bad. Circumstances happen in life that cause problems. Life happens - divorce, someone's death, moving, jealousy, new job. Everything from A to Z.

Somethings are better left alone. I think there are alot of people out there that take things to the grave. Do not hold a grudge, let it go, it's good for your health. Sometimes it is difficult to forgive when we are hurting from terrible things that happen to us. I even forgave my ex-husband. People will be people and do hurt each other. Forgiving someone is most beneficial to all of us. When we forgive our enemies or just rude and hurtful people, we begin to heal ourselves. Letting the anger go will make us feel lighter, healthier and happier.

For those of you who have not read *A Course in Miracles*, this is what is taught. Forgiveness and love is the key to living. We are all here to make the best choices for ourselves, so we can be at peace in heaven. (Some people have different names for heaven.)

One of John F. Kennedy's quotes: *"Forgive your enemies, but never forget their names."*

21

FREEDOM IS…
Free Will and Destiny

We can either choose free will for good or evil. Either one will tell what your destiny will be (freedom, jail or death), either for the good of people or to the detriment of people. John Wilkes Booth killed Abraham Lincoln. When he was caught, Booth was killed. Pope John Paul II was loved by people of all ages around the world. *What goes around comes around* is so true. Just watch the awful things people do to each other. Sit back and watch what happens to the people who hurt other people. Sometimes it is right in front of you when karma comes around and hands out punishment. Karma and destiny go hand in hand. I've never seen it to fail.

Free will gives us two choices: good or bad. There is no middle ground. Choices are either positive or negative. Our choices have good consequences or bad consequences. When you are not sure, ask a close friend, go to church, speak with your Mother, talk to your doctor. Ask people you can trust. Then make your decision.

My gut reaction must have been on vacation when I said yes to getting married. (Love is blind, but marriage was a great learning experience for me. I can help other people through their stuff because I have *been there, done that*. People ask me, if I would ever get married again?" My answer is, "I love my freedom."

22

FREEDOM IS…
Getting Yourself Unstuck

This is very important for everyone. It is the choices we make that will determine what we do in life. When you find yourself in a situation that is not to your liking, do something about it. Whether a bad marriage, a job that you do not like, maybe a move, etc. Just make a plan and make a move. Change your circumstances. Do it early in any game. Do not wait until you feel that it is too late for you to do anything for the better. Let go of the fear. It is never too late.

Being a prime example of this myself taking the first step was the hardest. Do it anyway. The next two, three steps make the next thousands of steps easier and easier. Try it you will see what I mean. What a freeing experience. Martina McBride sings a song called "Anyway." Nice song, listen to it.

I cannot say it enough for everyone to hear. Listen up people! Take responsibility for your life. Give yourself a gift. Just take that first step. What we want is inside of each one of us. Listen to yourself and the real you will appear. Life is meant to be fun and lived to the fullest. So, live it the best way that you can.

Here is one of my quotes: *"You are only stuck if you want to be."*

23

FREEDOM IS...
Giving Back

Volunteering is a great way to give back. When you do not have a lot of money to give to the organization, give your time, which will make you feel great. There are many organizations communities across the country. Go on the computer (http://charity navagiator.org/) or look in your phone book. Maybe there are some organizations in your neighborhood.

One of my customers said that her family members gave to help the homeless last year instead of giving each other gifts. They are going to do the same thing this year. What a wonderful thing to do. When more people get into giving back to their communities, people's circumstances will change for the better.

I will be giving back some proceeds of this FREEDOM IS book to benefit The Leary Firefighters Foundation (I love firefighters).

24

FREEDOM IS…
Government

The purpose of our government is to protect the people of the United States. James Madison put our "inalienable rights" in the Bill of Rights. Without laws, we would have total chaos. We are not a perfect government. As we go along, we will do better.

A suggestion: Bring dignity and kindness back to America. What I mean is that we have to have people in charge who are "class acts" and can do the job. (Dignity and kindness, does not mean that people are weak.) Being a class act means that they are human beings and want to be treated with dignity and kindness by their fellow Americans and people worldwide. Almost everyone on the planet likes to be respected and treated with dignity. Since John F. Kennedy, Martin Luther King and Robert F. Kennedy were killed, in my opinion, America has spiraled out of control. We would be a lot better to bring back what these three men stood for: equality, fairness, love of people, kindness, dignity, and people living their dreams. (I was one of the Youth For Kennedy in PA 1960).

Nowadays, you can easily be run down in a parking lot or shot for computer game. People get hurt on Black Friday (the start of the holiday season.) What's the point? All the stuff is material stuff. Sometimes it will break the same day you bought it. After the holidays (Christmas) there will be more in the stores for everyone to buy. There is plenty to go around. I like to give money, then people can buy what they really want or save the money for another day.

Man's inhumanity to man is alive and well and living everywhere. Let's bring kindness, equality, fairness, love of people and their dreams back in our lives and see how things start to turn around for the better. Remember, "What goes around really does come around."

The movie, *Bobby*, should be seen by everyone to really understand what I mean.

A few days ago, on the evening of December 26, 2006, Gerald Ford, at the age of 93, went home to God in heaven. President Ford was one of the class acts in Washington, DC. At the time of Watergate, this country was in turmoil, no one knew who to believe, not to believe, even Gerald Ford. Gerald Ford was a kind-hearted, common sense kind of man who led the country with dignity after that dark period of our history. He was just what the country needed at that time, a breath of fresh air. Isn't it something that all that Gerald Ford wanted to be in Washington, DC, was Speaker of the House? All of a sudden, he was Vice-President and then President of the United States. He was appointed Vice-President and President, never voted in for either position, and he was the best man for the job. The country needed his quiet wisdom, and I, for one, always will thank him for that. President Gerald R. Ford was a class act.

President Ford was also an athlete. He knew how to take a fall. Thanks to Chevy Chase, he was on *Saturday Night Live*, without being there. I am sure that Ford laughed, because a lot of times when he fell, he laughed at himself.

Whenever, I do something off-kilter (slip, trip, stumble), I am the first one to laugh at myself. When we think about things later, we usually laugh about it. So laugh out loud at yourself in the beginning and chuckle later. We should all not take ourselves so seriously. It wastes time and energy. It's just that simple!

25

FREEDOM IS...
Gratitude

I am so grateful for what I have and what I have had in my life. My parents and grandparents, my brother George Wensel, my cousin Dr. Tim Ryan, my uncle Ed Doyle, my uncle Howard Wensel. All the people that I have known, know now and will know have taught me lessons and will teach me more lessons. I have thanked them, and will thank the future people that I will meet in my journey throughout my life.

Even, the people who tried to hurt me, I have learned from them throughout my life. They will teach you great lessons. The best lesson is: never to deal with them again. Wish them well and move on with your life.

26

FREEDOM IS...
Harassment
Eliminated Forever

Harassment happens everyday on our planet. Whether at work, at home (neighborhood), or at play, it happens. Most of the people on this planet have had some type of harassment at sometime in their lives. Enough is enough. When someone starts to harass you there are steps that you can take.

At work, if it is your boss, talk to the corporate person who handles harassment. If another employee is harassing you talk to your boss before going to the corporate person. If you are part of a union, have a meeting with you boss and the shop steward and corporate to explain what is going on.

If nothing works: call the police, file a report, take photos if you can (some businesses have cameras), get in touch with the appropriate government office that handles harassment, call your attorney, file charges and sue. Some people may also choose to call the news media. They are always looking for a story such as harassment because so many people go through this worldwide.

Do not be afraid. No one is going to stick up for you, except you.

When you put the company on notice, then something will happen. The company may choose to settle with you or they will lie and say that only one person complained about the person or the harassment never happened. When this happens, just watch what happens to the one person who told the government agency that handles harassment that only one person complained or it never happened.

Remember, what goes around comes around. Sooner or later the one that lied and put in writing that the harassment did not happen or that only one person complained and signed the document will be hit by karma. It will come when they least expect it. Just sit back and watch.

Do the same thing if you are harassed at home or play. Call the police, file a report, get in touch with the government agency that handles harassment, take photos, call your attorney and sue.

Harassment is alive and well and living worldwide. The only way to stop it is to do something about it when it happens to you.

27

FREEDOM IS...
Helping Myself

Before I can help anyone else, I have to help myself. Being positive in all circumstances is the key to the life that I will live. It is not always easy, but do it, anyway, I tell myself. Martina McBride sings: "Anyway." If you haven't heard it, it's a great song with lots of heart.

And throughout the years, this is what I have done. This is what I will continue to do.

28

FREEDOM IS...
Humanitarianism

A portion of the proceeds from this Book/Journal will benefit The Leary Firefighters Foundation (I love firefighters).

Everyone that can, should lend a hand to helping someone in your community. Check out, "A Better Community.org." There are people everywhere who need help. So, get busy and lend a hand.

FREEDOM IS…
Immigration

We have laws on the books that we should enforce or update. Set the rules and stick to them. People want to come here and live in peace and freedom. Coming here legally will give you freedom. Being legal will give you more opportunities in America. Why would you want to keep looking over your shoulder in America? Why hide in America? That is not living free, that is living in fear. Hiding, and when found will give you a trip back home. What's the point?

Coming to America to be free and still not living totally free is a crime in itself. Life is great here. Americans want to help. Just ask for help.

30

FREEDOM IS...
Independence

It is not following the crowd. It's thinking for myself, having self-respect, being myself, taking "The Road Less Traveled" not being afraid to be myself. When you take care of yourself, then you can take care of other's much more easily.

Back in 1988 I thought I was going to die. My left side completely shut down. I could not feel anything from the top of my head to the tip of my toes on my whole left side. I told my future ex-husband that he was not going to work that day; he was taking me to the hospital. After a week in the hospital, (I could not even go out into the hallway), my family doctor at the time, Dr. William Cook, walked in and told me it was total stress. Since all the other tests were negative, he said, stress was the cause.

While I was in the hospital that week, and before I knew what the verdict was, I decided I was going to get rid of most of the stress in my life. So I made a list of what I was not going to do anymore. It took up three yellow legal pad sheets. Then, I made a list of what I was going to do. This was a 1 to 10 list that is still working to this day. I vowed that I would not get sick again, because of stress or anything else. It's working.

Some of the changes that I made were closing the outside business, fired my business partner, stayed at home for awhile, deciding what I wanted to do.

My motto is, "*If it's not fun (and legal) I am not doing it.*"

31

FREEDOM IS...
Individual

Live life without hurting other people. That is real freedom. When someone comes at you for any reason—harassment, bullying, threatening, abuse of any kind—you can take action because the other person came after you. But do it legally. Have dignity in what you do.

One of the best things I did in my life was my divorce. It made me totally free to be me. What fun! When I was married, I did live in fear. My ex threatened to take away one of the kids if I left him, but the kids were older when I divorced him. My ex was very verbally abusive and threatened my life. He did not want me to have a home business or an outside business. Enough was enough. There was a lot of money involved. I received a little over $20,500. I fired my attorney, went to the courthouse and did my own paperwork. The divorce cost me $50, including my name change. That was in 1998. It was a very good year.

Remember when I talked about karma and destiny? Two years after my divorce, my ex went to the doctor and was told by his doctor that he had cancer in six places. It had been almost 15 years earlier, to the day when I stood in the kitchen in Brookhaven, PA and told him that I would not be in the vicinity when a doctor would sit across the table from him and tell him that he has cancer. My future ex laughed right in my face. I did not know at that time he was going to have cancer in six places. (I was living in Las Vegas. I got the call from my daughter.) He was supposed to get married within a month, but the marriage never happened.

I tried to figure out why cancer in six places? Then, five years ago, I found out that my ex had terrorized our daughter and son throughout the years and told them that if they said anything to me, he would make it worse for them. At that time, I got the answer to my question. Remember, "What goes around comes around."

As a divorced woman, before I date anyone I have them checked out to see if they're telling me the truth. This saves a lot of time and energy and aggravation. This is my choice to safeguard myself.

Ladies and Gentlemen, tell the person (male or female) that you are going to have them checked out. They will either get really nervous and leave skid marks as they start for the door, or say that's all right with them. When you have them checked out, you will find out some really amazing things if they have lied. (Talk about Truth or Consequences) If you are thinking about the price (which is reasonable), do not be concerned; the answers you get are priceless.

Being true to me is my truth. I am certainly a challenge for anyone who dates me.

32

FREEDOM IS...
Inner Peace

Inner control of choice, spontaneity, fulfillment, and spirituality means being at peace, which means living without stress. Tai Chi or Yoga helps. Inner peace is knowing yourself. Know what you want and plan on how to get it, without hurting anyone else. Being strong enough to get through what life gives us. Some things are not easy to handle, but do it, anyway. Handle what you can handle in your life. Anything outside that does not pertain to you, just let it go. It has nothing to do with you. (Read the Serenity Prayer). Psychic Sylvia Browne always says, "Let go and let God" is the key.

There is so much stuff out there. Between computers, iPods, blackberries, now the iPhone, there is so much stuff that people could live four lifetimes and not be able to get to all the information just on the Web. Work, family, sickness take up a lot of time and being on the computer at work (playing and buying) can get your fired. So where does that put you? Just do what you can handle. Keep it simple.

Don't complicate your life. Life is not complicated it is easy. We (humans) are the ones who complicate our lives. Think about it.

33

FREEDOM IS...
Justice

Justice has two sides, good and evil. Justice happens when men and women trample on the rights of others. (killings, shootings, rapes). Most of the time, the people in jail belong there.

Sometimes some of the people in jail were framed and did not commit the crime. Nowadays, taking a person's DNA will separate the guilty from the not guilty.

Karma is part of justice. I call it God's helping hand on earth. The Final Justice at the Pearly Gates Belongs to God.

34

FREEDOM IS...
Keeping a Clear Head

When everything around you is going crazy, keep a clear head. It is not hard to do. It is easy to learn. When life gives you a lemon, make lemonade. When you get knocked down in life, screaming and hollering does not solve the problem. When you are finished screaming and hollering you still have the problem looking back at you. When emotions are involved a clear head is nowhere in sight.

Take the emotion out of the situation. Take the time to look for a solution. Think it through and the solution will come to you. Sometimes, putting the problem is God's hands (Let go and let God) is the answer. This works like a charm and you may get a phone call out of the blue and your problem is solved. This goes for every aspect of your life. It's just that simple.

FREEDOM IS...
Knowledge and Truth

Knowledge is education, but knowing what is really true is the key. As you know, I love the truth. I can deal with the truth. I cannot deal with a lie because it is not the truth. A lie will fester and grow.

A lie will grow and take all who are involved down with it. Stuff happens, and all the lies eventually end up on the news, on the Internet, and in court, and people either go to jail or are killed or their reputations are gone, families gone, jobs gone.

When someone is trying to tell me a lie, I know it. I will not always tell them that I know they are lying. But I will remember. Forgive, but don't forget.

When a person does something wrong, they should admit it. It is going to come out sooner or later. Sooner is better because later takes casualties along with it (families, workplaces, friends). Who wants to be a casualty? Knowledge of the truth will set you free. The American people are not stupid. We know a lie from the truth in anything from A to Z.

Mark Twain said "Always tell the truth; then you don't have to remember anything."

36

FREEDOM IS…
Laughter…Everyday

Laughing is always the best policy. There are some things in life that we cannot control. The weather, good or bad. How long will we have a certain job or career. Whether or not we will stay married. When a cancer cure will be found. Today, life can be trying, so try to live it as calmly as you can live your life.

Learn to laugh a lot. Laugh at the stupid things that happen. Laugh when you trip over your own feet. Laughter is good for you. When you have a bad day at work, unless its brain surgery, just laugh. Tomorrow is another day. In the scheme of things, make your life as simple as you can for yourself. Life is not complicated, we make it complicated. Remind yourself to keep it simple.

FREEDOM IS...
Laws

Laws are made to protect good people from bad people. Good actions bring happiness for people. Bad actions bring death or jail for the criminals and tragedy for its victims. Without laws, what would we have? Think about it. We would all be carrying guns or we would all be dead. It would be the Wild Wild West all over again.

Sometimes things look like they are out of control, and sometimes they are out of control, but right now it is the best we've got.

Think of ways to make it better. Change only starts with one person working together with other people. There are a lot of intelligent people in this country. One by one, we can keep the changes coming. Start changing things, its contagious.

38

FREEDOM IS…
Law of Attraction

This is something that works like a charm. Always be positive. In the midst of chaos, always be positive. There is an upside. Giving out positive thoughts and works keeps everything positive coming to you.

Giving out negative thoughts and words keeps everything negative coming to you. It's just that simple. When someone hurts you, thank them for doing it, they just taught you a lesson. Learn from it. Just ask for what you want and follow through with all the positive in your life. What you put out into the universe will come back to you, good or bad, I call it karma and destiny. You will see it in your life, and it will either be good or bad. It's just that simple.

Here is a quote from Florence Shinn, (1871–1940), "The game of life is the game of boomerangs. Our thoughts, deeds and words return to us sooner or later, with astounding accuracy."

39

FREEDOM IS...
Liberty

Our Founding Fathers loved freedom and liberty. This is so cool for all of us in America. Liberty and freedom started the whole thing. Wouldn't it be interesting to hear what the Founding Fathers would say and write in my Book/Journal?

One thing to see is the Statue of Liberty, which now a 120 years old. Thank you people of France. Take the boat ride around New York City and go to Ellis Island, where you may see your ancestors' names on the wall. If you are in New York for New Years Eve, go to Times Square. Do not miss it. If you only go one time you will never forget it. It's all very cool!

Visit Washington DC. Hot in the summer, cold in the winter. Go, anyway. See all the sights: Washington Monument, White House, Jefferson Memorial, Lincoln Monument, The Smithsonian, Arlington Cemetery (John and Jackie Kennedy burial site), Watergate Building, Kennedy Center for the Performing Arts. These are my favorites. Just love DC.

Visit Philadelphia, see the Liberty Bell, The Constitution Center, The Betsy Ross House, Independence Hall. Enjoy a Pat's Philly Cheese Steak and the Philly Soft Pretzels, Rita's Water Ice, Tasty Kakes and of course the Philly Phanatic (Mascot of the Philadelphia Phillies)

40

FREEDOM IS...
Life's Lessons

In life the good comes with the bad. I believe that we are all here for a reason. In order to get back to heaven, we all have to pass some tests. We all have choices and whether we pass or not pass the tests is up to us.

Life's lessons can be in your face. My dad had colon cancer. It was still hard and a lot of people were in shock. He died on January 5, 1985, the same day his mother died twenty years earlier.

Since my dad died of cancer, my mom sent her order to God. *Just let me go to sleep*. And she did (June 13, 1987). She was found on her screened front porch, lying on her chaise longe with her reading glasses on, and holding *The Enquirer* in her hands. What's better than that? Mom got her wish.

I was on vacation with my family in Rehoboth Beach, DE. We were at five o'clock Mass on Saturday night and a cold wind came around me. I knew that something had happened, that Mom was gone. She was such a good lady. Even the men at the post office in Brookhaven, PA, cried when they found out she had died. Everyone who knew her loved her. She certainly got her wish. Our family doctor, Dr. William Cook, called me to let me know that she had a brain aneurysm, which is a bulge in a blood vessel in the brain. Aneurysms most commonly occur in arteries at the base of the brain.

Our family psychic friend Bob said that Mom went straight to heaven. She was such a special person, he did not know anyone who went to heaven as fast as Mom went to heaven. How cool is that?

Two events happened after Mom passed into heaven.

A few months after Mom died, I knew she was in heaven, since I am a Taurus, I still wanted to know. One early morning (3 AM) I woke up and with the bedroom door closed there was a bright light in the hallway. "*What is that?*" I thought. So, I got up and went to the door. When I opened the bedroom door it looked like the sun was in my hallway. That is really something, since no one left any lights on in the hallway. So, when I looked, I could not see any pictures on the walls, but the light was so bright I thought I needed my sun glasses on.

Then, I saw her. No, it was not my Mom that I saw. It was the Blessed Mother, dressed in a pale blue mantle and white robes. Absolutely beautiful. She told me that my Mom was fine and happy. A great peace came over me. The Blessed Mother smiled. I could not see through her. She was in human form. Then in a few seconds the hallway was back to normal and I could see the pictures on the wall again. I was fine and went back to sleep. After all it was 3:05 AM. (This is good karma)

In the morning my future ex asked me what was the bright light in the hallway during the night. He said it was as bright as the sun. I just smiled and said, "The Blessed Mother said Mom was fine and happy."

A few months later Padre Pio came to visit. My mom was a big fan of Padre Pio. This time it was no bright light in the hallway. It was a 2 AM meeting at my kitchen table. How cool is that? He stayed about twenty minutes. The Padre did most of the talking. I just listened. Padre sat at the table in his brown robe and sandals. Looked just like his pictures. What amazed me was I could not see through him, because he was in his human body. (This is good karma)

In October 1989 my brother Brian's Wedding was in the Chicago area. Three things happened. The first was flying from Philadelphia to Chicago. The flight was fine until we were landing at O'Hare Airport. We were very close to the ground when the pilot pulled the nose of the plane upward (it felt like we were going straight up) and then leveled out, circled a few more times. Now, once again, trying to land. I thought here we go again. As we were coming in for the second landing the same thing happened again. Very close to the ground we had to pull up and go around again. We either almost hit something, or something almost hit us. I guess the third time is a charm, the landing was fine. I told the pilot that I would like to get to my brother's wedding alive and in one piece. Thank you, God.

At Brian and Emily's Wedding - Feelings are usually real and true.

During the wedding, Clare, Georges' wife was reading one of the scriptures. Suddenly, when she looked up toward the choir, and I saw the look on Clare's face, I knew Mom was standing in the choir. Mom was standing there smiling, watching Brian and Emily get married. How cool was that? Clare and I were the only one's to see Mom in the choir loft. People asked me if I ever get scared when I see people that are no longer alive. No, it is not the people who are living in heaven that we should fear. They have been here and they want us to do well and join them on the other side.

What's scary are the people that are alive who will do us harm? Think about it!

The real shocker was the death of my brother George Wensel. George, his two sons, my daughter, and a number of cousins and friends were at the Outer Banks, NC at a Family Reunion in July,

1995. (Before George went on vacation, I asked him why he was not taking the boys to Disney World or anywhere else on the planet, besides going on a vacation with those people (cousins). George said that he wanted the boys to get to know the cousins. (What they know now they will never forget.) George was vice-president of NEP INC. in Pittsburgh, PA. He had a great technical mind in the field of TV Sports. At the reunion at the Outer Banks, NC, he drowned. But there was always something very strange about George's death. Someone said that George was trying to save his two sons when he drowned. Wrong! A female cousin started hollering. Why? There was nothing wrong. No one was in trouble. (This female always hollered before she was hurt, anyway) Brent was on his boogie board in the water and Colin was on the beach with my daughter. Karen knew where everyone was on the beach and in the water. His sons were not in trouble and George was not saving anyone. George was standing in ankle deep water holding a boogie board. Then a male cousin who was standing in back of George was holding the same boogie board that George held. George was face down in the water. Brent came out of the water on his boogie board and said to Karen his Dad was not moving and he thought he was dead. There are so many unanswered questions about Georgie's death. George could have not gotten to where he was in his life by doing something stupid. How can you drown when you are in ankle-deep water? George was a big man. A lot of questions were never answered.

There was no explanation on this planet for my aunt's and uncle not going to their nephew's funeral in Pittsburgh, PA. There were, also, some cousins that did not go either. I am sure that when Mom's sister and brother-in-law died, she met them at the Pearly Gates and asked them, "Why didn't you go to George's funeral? Even if Mom knew the answer (which she probably did) she would want to hear it from them. If they did see the white light and did not get to go through the Pearly Gates, then they are in Purgatory for an extended part of time, though they will eventually get through the Pearly Gates. If by chance, they are in neither place, then Mom will never see them because they have taken the red escalator into Hell.

When I called George's psychic friend Bob, he told me George had been there and he was not happy with the cousins. I think not. He could see how they were treating my daughter and his two sons. This was not good. I usually have a gut sense of what is going to happen, not this time. I asked our psychic friend, *"why did I not sense anything?"* He answered, *"because it was not his time to go."*

Always believed that things are meant to be 98% of the time. The other 2% is. *"What just happened?"*

It was a good thing that my daughter was there with George's two sons. I called my daughter and there was a pizza party going on in the house. This was Tuesday night, George died a few hours earlier.

Clare, the boys mother came to pick them up on Wednesday morning. All, except my daughter, decided since they paid $500.00 for the week they were going to stay until Friday and go sight-seeing. My daughter could not believe what she was seeing. They would not let her into the house for 24 hours, the house that George, his sons and my daughter were staying in. My question was why? I called and told them that if they did not let her in I was going to call the police. She finally got into the house and took a shower.

On Thurday morning around 9 AM, Karen drove alone (no one was allowed to drive home with her), out of the Outer Banks, north on I-95 toward PA. (Here was the girl who worked for her Uncle George on Golf Tournaments and the Tour DuPont, driving alone in George's Green Explorer with a broken heart.) She stopped at a friend's house near DC. Then, she continued on north on I-95, arrived at home around 10PM Thursday night. She was exhausted.

We left Friday morning for George's Funeral in Pittsburgh.

My brother Brian and I did not want the cousins at the funeral. They came anyway. And yes, they went sight-seeing in Pittsburgh. I was asked if it was ok for them to go sight-seeing? I told them I did not care what they did. I did not want them there anyway.

At the Funeral Mass, I was the last one to speak about George. It was really very hard and very easy at the same time. Everyone wanted to know what he was like as a child. What you saw was what you got. This was George, all through his life. George never changed. He was the same extremely intelligent little boy that grew into a very brilliant wonderful man. Blond hair, blue eyes, 200 lbs., 6'5." He was like a big teddy bear. He would give me big bear hugs.

When I asked the cousins what they saw, they said nothing. That is not a hard question. When I asked the aunts what their children saw, my mothers' sisters said nothing. They all had blank looks on their faces. If you saw something, say so. If you saw nothing, say so. Saying nothing at all told me a lot.

I came really close to throwing the cousins out of the church. I am sure it would have made the headlines, if I through them out of the church. I was standing there talking about George, and knowing that they were sitting there really ticked me off. I thought, *"What would George do?"* I decided to let them stay. As I said before, karma is alive and well and living everywhere.

Like everything else in life, at some point the answer will come. Some things just boggle the mind and take longer for the answers to come. Remember, *"You can pick your friends, but you can't pick your relatives."*

My family has really gone from large to small. My brother Brian and his wife Emily, my daughter Karen and son Ed, Brent and Colin Wensel, 4 King Charles Spaniels and a Chocolate Lab. Life is good.

Most people who knew George loved him. He was part of sports around the world—the Olympics (summer and winter), the Breeders Cup, NASCAR, NBA, NFL, ESPN, HBO, CBS, NBC, the Americas Cup, Wimbledon. Whatever the sports venue, George was a part of it. George was also part of the Academy Awards, Dick Clark music award shows and other shows.

Most people who knew George loved him. There were a few that were jealous of him and his accomplishments; but the majority of people who knew George just loved him. George had one of the biggest funerals in Pittsburgh's history. hroughout the years, people who only met George once, remembered him and came to his funeral. He made such an impression on people they had to pay their respects to George. People came from around the world, a lot of them because they could not believe that George was gone. George treated everyone the same. Whether you were the president of NBC or the person who parks the cars, George treated everyone with respect and kindness.

I was asked what people should do to remember George. I told them, "Just to treat people like George treated people and love you kids, like George loved his two sons." The people who knew George will never forget George.

I will say that George did everything that he wanted to do in his 37 years on this earth. How many people can say that and know it to be true?

The National Academy of Television Arts and Sciences – Sports Emmy Awards – instituted The George Wensel Technical Achievement Award.

On December 11, 2007 George Wensel was among the first eleven people inducted into the Inaugural Class of the Hall of Fame for Sports Broadcasting and Technology Executives. Brent and Colin Wensel received the award in their father's honor.

Additional remarks regarding Karma.

My future ex was not that broken up that my brother died. George was going to come from Pittsburgh and have a chat with my future ex about his treatment of me. A day after George died, I was standing at the dining room table and my future ex came down the hallway and said, "Well, I guess your brother will not be coming to talk to me now?" I, turned, and said, "Don't kid yourself. Now you won't see him coming." And my ex has seen George, quite often throughout the years. Remember, "What goes around comes around." (This is bad karma regarding my ex)

A few months after George was buried I got a call from my Aunt Honey. She wanted me to come over and talk. So, I stopped by and we sat at her kitchen table. She went on to tell me that she was really upset about what was going on. I sat and said *nothing*, but thought, *"what's going on?"*

She was upset because every morning George would be standing at the bottom of all the cousins beds when they awoke. Just amazing, because they live in different states. George, also, sat in the back seat of their cars when they were driving. There were other things that she did not mention.

It took all I could do not to role on the floor laughing. I dug my nails into the palms of my hands to keep from laughing. I said nothing. What could I do about it? I left and laughed all the way home. I know it went on for a long time. I am not sure if it is still going at this time. But, who knows? (This is bad karma on their part)

About four months after George died, my Aunt Honey called and was talking about George and said that he was not around much anyway. I could not believe what I just heard. (It is ok that he is dead because he was not around much anyway) What is that? She has a son who lives in the southwest. He only visits once a year. (I would have never said that about her son.) When George was alive he visited many times throughout the year.

My mother and brother George were up in heaven listening to this stuff. I'm done. Enough, already!

There was always some jealousy there with my aunt. Like a competition between the cousins. What's that about? Everyone chose different occupations. George's name was always on the TV credits at the end of sports shows, music shows, Academy Awards. My brother Brian's name is on the Movie credits at the end of the motion pictures.

Remember, when I spoke about making a decision. I made a decision and it was done. I wished my aunt well and did not deal with her negativity again. The next time I saw her was at her funeral. (This was bad karma on her part)

About six months after George died, I received a phone call from my friend Rosalyn. She said the night before someone broke into her apartment and tried to attack her.

Months before I had sent a photo of George to her and as she looked at George's photo, she hollered, "George help me." All of a sudden the guy who was on top of her, was lifted off of her and thrown against the wall. Just amazing, since there were only two people in the room. (Rosalyn and the attacker)

Rosalyn said "George saved her life." George always liked Rosalyn. She said people do come back to help. We cannot always see them but they are there. (This is Roslyn's good karma)

Seems like it is karma to me. Remember, what goes around comes around.

FREEDOM IS...
Living Your Dreams

Dream as big as the sky! The sky is endless. Do not let the detractors take your dreams away from you. Have your own thoughts and lay no claim on other people's thoughts. Think for yourself. Dreams can be fulfilled at any age. Age is just a number. Work on what you know. What is your passion? What would you like to do more than anything in the world? Think about it. Only you know what you really want to do and not do. Remember, "Dreams never retire, neither should you."

Look at me, I did not know I was going to write a Book/Journal until I started to write the Book/Journal. Who knew? (only the man upstairs and his friends knew.)

42

FREEDOM IS…
Lost

People who do not pay attention will lose their freedom very easily. Sometimes people are born into slavery and it takes them time to get their freedom. Freedom should be at the top of everyone's list of things to keep.

Without freedom everything is lost. Being complacent is not the right thing to be.

Live your life to the fullest. Be aware of what is around you when you are out and about, but do not stress out. Just have fun. Your gut reaction will serve you well. Anything that looks suspicious to you, call the police, FBI and Homeland Security.

Example: If it walks like a duck, talks like a duck, it's a duck! Meaning, if something doesn't look quite right, it probably isn't.

Millions of people have cell phones. Use yours to call the police. Stay calm, stay away from the package, box, car, truck, whatever led you to this gut reaction. Just go with it. It works every time. Just listen to your gut reaction.

We all have to keep each other safe. When it comes down to the basics, we are all on this planet to help each other. It's just that simple!

Sometimes, during your life you will feel lost. You are not sure what to do next. You are going in twenty different directions. Make good choices. Just keep going into your future.

FREEDOM IS...
Mind Control

Most of the time, (except when I was writing this book) I control my own mind. I throw out all the trash in the rooms of my mind. Keep your own thoughts, not other people's thoughts. Stay focused on the good stuff in my life and what I want to accomplish. There is so much information out there that is not true. Keep a positive mind. Our minds get so cluttered, it's a wonder that our heads don't explode. Sort out what you think and throw the rest away.

Some customers of mine do not watch any news or read newspapers. They are happy in their lives not knowing a lot of the rhetoric. They are really happy campers.

Me, I was a political science major, sociology major, and management minor at Widener University. I am always interested in politics. I don't always like the antics, so I just read between the lines.

44

FREEDOM IS…
Music

Without music in our lives, what would it be? *Boring*!!! Think about it. No Waltzs. No Beatles. No Country. No Jazz. No Rap. No Musicals. No Beach Boys. No Dick Clark (world's oldest teenager). No Rock and Roll. No music, that would be criminal.

I love all kinds of music. I love to dance. Rock and Roll is in my soul and always will live there. (American Bandstand was fifty years old on August 5, 2007.) Thank you, Dick Clark.

A few dances I have to do is to dance down Broadway and the Las Vegas Strip. What fun!

45

FREEDOM IS…
Never Give Up

Sometimes it is easier to give up and just to sit there and do nothing. What does that get you? Nothing! I am a Taurus and I am really the Bull. Go for what you want (always legal) which keeps you out of trouble.

The world is so out of kilter nowadays, but we have to keep focused on what we want for ourselves and for our freedom. Remember, never, never, never give up.

46

FREEDOM IS...
Opportunity

America is certainly the land of opportunity for the majority of the world. People come from Rwanda, India, China, Mexico to get away from genocide, poverty, and any other oppressions. People from around the world have been coming the America since the 17th century. This is a wonderful thing.

My mom's parents (William & Delia Creighton Garvey) came from County Mayo, Ireland. My grandfather was a school teacher in Ireland, a very smart man. He always had a book in his hands. He just loved to read and learn. My grandfather came to America first, then, my grandmother followed him. They had the same thing to say when they saw the Statue of Liberty in New York Harbor. They both said, it was one of the most beautiful sites they ever saw. Liberty brings hope for everyone who comes to this wonderful land. Their names are now on the wall of Ellis Island. What a sight to see. I could feel them standing there, smiling.

Opportunity is everywhere in America. This is a fun country. Americans like to help people. This is what we do best. People come here for a better life. Most people just want to live in peace and harmony, not continually fighting. They want to work, raise their children, learn, start a business, get married, stay single, enjoy themselves. Life is too short for anything else. Keep it simple!

47

FREEDOM IS...
Pay It Forward

Part of the funds from the sale of the Book/Journal will benefit The Leary Firefighters Foundation (I love firefighters). Denis Leary is the President. Watch – "Rescue Me."

In just about every city and town in the country there are fire-houses. Without them, what would we do? More lives and buildings would be lost. They risk their lives everyday for us. So, funds will bnefit the Leary Firefighter's Foundation.

Whatever we can do the help each other - Just Do It! Helping gives you an extra charge in your heart. Help year round, not just at holiday time.

━━━━━━━━━━━━━━━━━

FREEDOM IS…
Peace

Let's bring peace back to the planet. Let's not talk about war, let's talk about peace. What's wrong with Peace. Some people would say that there is no money in Peace. Maybe, not! But it beats the alternative. Nobody is taking any money with them, anyway. John Lennon's song "Give Peace a Chance." Why not do it?

There is so much negativity out there. On TV, the Newspapers, Internet, there is so much negativity, maybe negative sells; but negative does not solve any problems, it causes problems. Instead of talking about war, things would change for the positive when we talk about Peace.

John Lennon's song "Imagine" everyone living in peace worldwide.

49

FREEDOM IS...
Personal Success

Almost everyone wants personal success. The thought of doing something well, the thought of having more of what you want, (without hurting other people), just being kind to people—all this is personal success. Help mothers and children and fathers succeed in life. Help them all on the street or in shelters, or in your neighborhoods. Don't always think about what we want for ourselves. That's like spending the Christmas money just on yourself and not buying gifts for anyone else. When you help others, you will get what you want. It's just that simple!

The key to happiness is helping others. When you see the mother's and children smile, it's priceless. Just holding a door for someone (male or female) is personal success.

My dad worked for Scott Paper Company for forty-three years. (He just loved making paper). He always helped family members, friends, and neighbors when they needed his help. Dad could fix any car, electric problem, fence, different parts of the house, garden, sidewalk, almost everything from A to Z. Whatever it was he knew just what to do.

What I look at now is how many people are really going to work at the same company for forty-three years? I think not. Most people will have at least five different employers in their lifetime. It seems to me that loyalty in not there anymore. This is why we have to take care of ourselves. We have to depend on ourselves.

Mom helped people in different ways. She worked outside the home throughout the years in real estate and accounting. She helped with money, food, good thoughts and kindness. She helped her sisters, brothers, friends, neighbors, and strangers. When they needed her, Mom was there with a smile. Some people take kindness for weakness. Mom was kind and also strong in what she did. When we did something wrong, she would let us know with kindness and a reason why, and we did not do it again.

50

FREEDOM IS…
The Press

We should have the freedom to say what is the truth. What's wrong with the truth? The truth comes out sooner or later. Years ago, books were burnt. That is hiding what is true. Getting the real important stories out to the people is the key. Stories that can help peoples lives.

The integrity of all the media (TV, Internet, newspapers, radio) is the key component to knowing what is true. Americans can read between the lines and know the truth from a lie. We have gotten really good at distinguishing between the two. Working in a supermarket helps to get an insight on what people are thinking. They will come out and tell me. Most people are pleasant and want to talk about themselves and what is in the news. I usually have a positive answer for them to help them with their situations. I have been there, done that and can give the advice that they need to hear and use in their lives.

51

FREEDOM IS...
Privacy

It is one's own spirit. What we say or do, how we handle different situations, that's how other people see us. People want their privacy, especially after sitting in a long line of traffic, having a bad day at work. They close the door behind them, kick off their shoes, shed their clothes, run bath or shower, and get all the bad vibes and grime of the day off themselves. That works for me.

Maybe there are some days when I just want to stare at the TV, work on my books, or sleep. It's my choice. People who go about their lives and just want to have peace are part of this group.

We now live in a different time. Everything changed on September 11, 2001. People now look at things differently. They figure it happened and probably will happen again. Our freedoms have changed to keep us safe. This is for the betterment of all of us. Being aware of what is around us is the key now.

Then there is the other group, who are ready to cause problems for many of people. Tabs have to be kept on them to see what they are up to. This is for the safety of the other people who want peace in their lives. I like cameras everywhere.

In Las Vegas, cameras are everywhere. Millions of cameras should be in every town and city across America. This would stop crime from happening or at least slow it down. If you are not doing anything wrong, why would you care? If you are cheating, robbing, killing, then you have something to really worry about. Who wants to be in those groups? Not me! Cameras are good. People, go about your business and live your lives every day!

52

FREEDOM IS...
Quite Serenity

Take time to really smell the roses. It's good for your health, your head, your heart, your psyche. Step back and look around and take a good look at what you are seeing. You may see something that you did not see before or had not really seen for years. It may really surprise you.

I have been doing this for years. When I ended up in the hospital in 1988, I made up my mind that I was going to take care of myself first. This is not being selfish. If I did not take care of myself, how could I take care of anyone else?

Knowing who I am, what I believe and how I treat other people and live my life is a comfort to me. Take each day and go with the flow. I can make plans for the future and taking each day and living it to the fullest will get me to my future plans. The Book/Journal was a future plan that is becoming a present reality.

53

FREEDOM IS…
Relationships

Relationships are sometimes hard to deal with. At home, at work, at school, at play, in families…sometimes it is hard to define. Most times, people agree to disagree. It is important to keep balance in your life, like doing different things is part of life, like not eating the same thing everyday. People do not want to be bored.

Sometimes life is strange, sometimes fun, sometimes sad. What am I here for? But it's all part of life. If a relationship is bad, get away from that relationship as soon as you can. Be good to yourself. Take care of your kids, save yourself from lots of heartache. Life is a test. We make good and bad choices. How we handle our choices is the key to how we will end up in life and in death. Put yourself first, then you can handle the rest of the stuff that goes on.

Knowing who you are first, will put you on your lifes plan - stay true to who you are in your life.

54

FREEDOM IS…
Religion and Dialects

In the United States, different religions are working together for the betterment of mankind. We are all here on earth to get back to heaven. People have different versions of heaven, but people strive to get back there when they die. Whether you turn to Jesus, Mohammad, Allah, or Buddha, unless you are an atheist, (God even loves the atheists), most people believe in a higher power.

Robert, who now lives in heaven, had a friend who was an atheist. She said that there was nothing after life. Robert said there was a heaven. Robert told his friend to let him know what she thought when she passed. When she came back she told Robert he was right about heaven. I am sure that they talked about it when Robert arrived at the Pearly Gates.

God only knows who will get back into heaven. God is just, and I believe that if a person is good and lives a good life, whether he or she is a believer or not, God will open the Pearly Gates of heaven for them.

I know a lot of good people across the country. They want to live their lives in peace, prosperity, and love. I have traveled through most of the fifty states. We have a great country. People are people. Besides different religions, there are also different types of speech (dialects) in America, from New England (listen to Senator Ted Kennedy) to New York/New Jersey lingo (*you talkin' to me?*) to Philadelphia (*yo, yo, yo!*). No matter where I go in the country, people always knew I was from the Philadelphia area. This is pretty funny, since I do not think I have a Philly accent, but I will admit to it, because other people hear my Philly accent. Everybody's from somewhere.

Whether from Virginia to Florida's Southern drawl, to New Orleans and Nashville (country music voices), West Virginia and Kentucky, up through the Midwest to Chicago to the Southwest, including Texas (*y'all – you all*) and all the Mountain States with their twang—I love all the different dialects in this country. This is what makes America great. California (Mexican, Asian), Oregon and Washington have (mostly normal dialects).

I love this country with all its differences. No wonder, people want to come to America, they have come here to live in freedom. They all will bring a certain flavor to this country.

Anyone who comes to America learn the English language. Knowing the language makes it easier to live and get around where you live and to ask for help.

55

FREEDOM IS...
Responsibility

I am responsible for my own actions. The blame game stops with me. When I look in the mirror, I was the one who made the choices for me. Taking responsibility is part of freedom. People should not blame others. What's the point? The real truth always comes out. The only one responsible for me getting into heaven is me. I will only be judged on what I do, not for what anyone else does.

Responsibility (character) is the backbone of a person. It shows what each one of us is made of, whether we like it or not. Taking responsibility is not easy for a lot of people; but in the long run it is the best thing to do. For example, if you are a cheater of any kind (say you cheated on your wife or husband), it is going to come out. If you hurt someone (driving a car while drunk, being a harasser at school, harasser at work, anything), apologize, make amends, go to jail, community service. Taking responsibility for ourselves is the first step; the next step gets easier. Try it. You will like it.

Whatever it takes to make amends. The TV show, *My Name Is Earl* is about a man who took advantage of the whole town, stealing, lying through out the years. Now he has a list of all the bad things that he ever did to the people in his town. Now he wants to give back to the people he hurt throughout the years. As he makes amends, Earl crosses the names off of his list. Some people are receptive, some are not; but, Earl is taking responsibility for all his actions and trying to make amends, one person at a time.

56

FREEDOM IS...
Second Chances

Almost everyone should have a second chance, unless the person is a robber, rapist, murderer, that is another story, no second chances. I do not believe in five, ten, twenty, fifty or a hundred chances. People are human and make mistakes and should be given a second chance if they deserve a second chance.

When a person is late for work, late for a date, tied up in traffic (this has probably happened to many of us) or late for an appointment, other individuals will make the call on the severity of losing the first chance in order to be given a second chance. Examples: Calling in sick, and then your face shows up on the television screen as part of the audience of a sports event or TV show. Being seen by someone from the office going into an interview at another company. Worse, a cheating husband or wife being caught by the other spouse or a private investigator. (*Gotcha*)

57

FREEDOM IS...
Self-Discipline...Adult

Discipline is not being mean or vindictive to yourself. If you were not disciplined as a child, it's a new lesson for you as an adult It is disciplining yourself to be on time for church, for work, for lunch, for dinner, for the movies, for anything, etc. Discipline teaches us from an early age how to become a productive citizen. It gets you where you are going on time. Being undisciplined, you are always late, always behind. Buy a clock for each room. Make sure they work. Check the one in your car. Wear a watch that works. Make it easy for yourself.

If you were not disciplined as a child: Setting limits and objectives is part of getting yourself where you want to be with your dreams and your destiny. When you are disciplined, you will have more time to do things you want to do without running late. It's funny how discipline works. It really gives you more free time for everything else in your life. Just do it. It's good for you. Disciplining yourself gives you freedom.

If we do not discipline ourselves, others will have to discipline us. It's guaranteed that we will not like their discipline or where we end up. (prison, hospital, dead)

━━━━━━━━━━━━━━━━

FREEDOM IS…
Self-Realization

This is realizing what you really want and how you are going to get what you want, legally. Sometimes we have to invent ourselves and reinvent ourselves throughout our lifetime. Whatever is not working for the positive, make a change from the negative to the positive.

We have to look inside ourselves so we are not brainwashed by outside influences.

We have to bring our whole self together, bring out our personality. It is part of our true self. Your real spirit will shine through. Wait till you see what happens.

Self-Realization gives me freedom. Self-Realization gives you freedom.

———————————————

FREEDOM IS...
Simplicity

Make it simple. Always. Since I have gotten all the stuff that I did not want to do out of my life, everything is simple. My list of ten is still working and I know everyone's list of ten will be different from mine.

Whatever works for you in your life, keep it. Whatever is not working for you, change it. Without making a change for the better, nothing will change for the better.

Everyone is different with different needs and wants in their lives. Again, whatever works for you in your life, go for it, see how it works for you. Example: If you have clutter in your house, garage, attic, get rid of it. It you have not used it, worn it, ridden it for a year, it needs to go. Sell it, give it away, or throw it away. It will make you feel great! Just to see the extra space you have in your house will be a treat for you.

Months before my divorce was final I called Goodwill to come and take a ton of things away. They were all good things people could use. It was a treat for me to see the Goodwill Truck pull up and take all that stuff away. I waived goodbye to the Goodwill Truck as it pulled away with a big smile on my face. Freedom at its best.

Whatever does not work, make a change for the better. When you get all the excess junk, crap, stuff out of your life, see how much simplicity you now have in your life. You are going to love it. You will wonder why you didn't do this before. Simplicity stops chaos.

60

FREEDOM IS...
Freedom From Slavery

Holding people back from what they can be is not freedom for them, but freedom by the one who holds them captive and in fear. Abraham Lincoln freed the slaves in the United States. Slavery still exists around the world. People should be free to be what they can be. Man was born free. We should all want to keep it that way.

To be free is a struggle, but it is certainly worth it. What's better than freedom? Think about it. Slavery is still going on around the world (slave labor is still alive). Slavery will eventually lead to freedom.

61

FREEDOM IS…
Social Change

Speak up. One person can make a difference, one person at a time. Nothing happens overnight. People are responsible for social change. Nonconformists are the ones who make changes. They do not follow the crowd. People have rights. We have come a long way in 232 years and we still have a long way to go. Moving forward is fun for all of us.

Get back to the right thing to do. Treat everyone the same. Every one of us likes to be treated with respect. When someone does not treat us with respect, we get upset. Put yourself in the other person's shoes. When they are disrespected, they get upset, too. Social change is freedom.

We are all on this planet together. Start treating each other with respect. Start getting along and stop fighting each other. What's the point?

I do not see any transportation going to other planets, do you? If there was, I am sure there would be a long line of people waiting to get on board. Maybe, some with one-way tickets. Remember, the Broadway Show, "Stop the World I Want To Get Off." Earth is where it is for all of us at this point. So, get along people!

62

FREEDOM IS...
Spirituality

This is the peaceful acceptance of reality. We are all spiritual beings, whether all of us believe this or not.

When some things happen, good or bad, our spirit (or as some people call it our gut) will react. Example: for Eagle fans, when Donovan McNabb was hurt in November 2006, all the spirit went out of that game. Unfortunately, the Eagles lost. Their fans were down, but a new turnaround happened with Jeff Garcia and the Eagles began to win.

Spirituality is fixing myself first. Healing myself is the key. Then I can help other people. It takes feeling and thinking. Being a perfectionist. I have been there, done that. It's not good for me. It put me in the hospital in 1988.

Some days, it is not easy to keep your spirit up, but do it, anyway. It's good for you. Remember, to laugh. It's good for your health. Spirituality is Freedom.

63

FREEDOM IS…
Speech

I believe in free speech. If I did not have free speech, this "Book/Journal with a Twist" would have probably not happened. Everyone good or evil, should be able to speak. Whether we agree or not agree, this is America and free speech is spoken here.

Free speech is great when it helps people, but when free speech goes after groups of people with a negative tone, that is not helping anyone. That is going to hurt someone or a lot of people. We live in America where people can speak their minds and when people cause a problem, justice takes over and they go to jail.

With our freedom of choice we can also click the dial to turn the speeches off. Love that remote! Free Speech is freedom.

64

FREEDOM IS...
Sports

I like all kinds of sports. My favorite sport is golf. All the golfers are pretty decent people and are very good in what they do while practicing and playing in the different tournaments.

The other sports are basketball, football, baseball, soccer, tennis. My favorite football team is Notre Dame. Sitting in the rain, snow, sleet and hail is fun in South Bend, Indiana. The team plays their hearts out on that field. I was in the stands, but I felt like I was on that field. Its always a hoot to go to a Notre Dame game.

NASCAR is also a favorite of mine. When sitting in the stands, you can feel the power of the cars going around the track. It is really amazing. Fun, fun, fun. Everyone should attend a NASCAR race.

65

FREEDOM IS...
Struggle

Not everyone worldwide is free. Think of China, North Korea, Venezuela, Iran, Darfur. Not everyone has the freedom to think, to choose, to live. Freedom is not easy, but respect for ourselves and others set us free. The majority of people are good people. They just want to live their lives in peace and freedom.

There are people who do not want other people to be free. They want to control people, threaten people, kill people. This is what they do. Freedom is not on their agenda. They are afraid of freedom.

This is a real shame. With a little common sense, even those leaders who do not like freedom would have more freedom. They would trust more people and delegate the good work for the whole country and everyone could be free, the country would be thriving, people would be happy. Think about this. What a concept!

66

FREEDOM IS...
Thought and Opinion

Most people have opinions, whether we like them or not. Thought is a part of a person's soul, who they truly are. This is a good thing. I am one who speaks her mind.

You can say how you feel without hurting people. You can say things with a smile, be forthright and kind. Most people want to know the truth. Without the truth, what do you have? Lies. Confusion.

Oprah has a great response, "When someone shows you their true self, believe them."

67

―――――――――――――――――――

FREEDOM IS...
TRUSTS

To protect you, your family and your things, put what you have in a Trust. Most of the wealthy people have everything in a Trust.

If you are not wealthy, you can still have a Trust. Many people do not realize this fact. If you are threatened with a lawsuit and everything is in a Trust, what is there to take?

Look into it. Check with your favorite attorney.

FREEDOM IS...
Unique

Being unique is being different. Start a business (Internet or storefront), volunteer, help a child, help a neighbor, help a stranger. (It makes your heart sing)

Everything on the planet was made or invented by a unique person. What was made or invented benefits millions of people. What is your new invention?

Fear keeps us stuck, stops us from moving ahead. Stop being afraid. Just do it! When we all work together that is being a unique group of people.

What makes you Unique?

69

FREEDOM IS...
Vision

Know what you want and have the vision to plan it out. Always do it legally (jail in not cool, freedom is better), so you can achieve your dreams. Keep positive people around you all the time.

Send the negative people away. Get any form of negativity out of your life. Step by step, you can do this. One step at a time.

My brother George was a great visionary in Sports TV. A lot of what you see today George put into place when he was alive.

FREEDOM IS...
Volunteering

What fun! Do what you can do to help your neighbors, friends and people that you do not know. There are organizations all over the United States and around the world. Check out the ones in your town or city. Spend an hour or two each day that you can give your time.

Believe me, it is time well spent. When you see the smile on a person's face that you have helped, it will make you feel so alive and happy. Remember, karma can slap you or hug you.

Do what you can. If you can hammer a nail, paint a wall, lay carpeting, go and do it. If you can cook, lend a hand to older citizens in your neighborhood, run errands for them, whatever you can do to help. If you cannot give the time, give some money. Just do it!

71

FREEDOM IS...
Women and Men

Women and men are not equal. Men make more money than women. Women were granted the right to vote, to work.

Take it from me, women's rights begin in their souls. Their spirits rise to the occasion. I got out of a bad situation (marriage), and I am not going to get into another one. Stay focused and move ahead.

It will be a very interesting time in this country when there is the first female President of the United States in the White House. It could happen. We now have Nancy Pelosi, the new Speaker of the House.

FREEDOM IS…
Why People Come To America

People travel hundreds and thousands of miles to come to America for freedom not because they do not have anything else to do that day. It takes time and energy to travel a short distance, never mind from all over the planet. (Since I have traveled in most of the states, I know it takes time and energy to travel.)

When people come from all different parts of the planet, it is sometimes a culture shock for them. There is a language different (words like "cool," "what a hoot," "in your face"), trying to fit in, going to school. So much to choose from: food, clothing, shopping malls, everything from A to Z.

Happily, the people learn the process and become productive citizens and prosper in this country, just like our ancestors did. Welcome to each and everyone of our new citizen's.

73

FREEDOM IS…
Your Freedoms

We will all take responsibility for our freedoms. Do the best for ourselves and our love ones. We do not know when we will have a job or not or whether there will be any money left in the Social Security fund. Some will get the money, others will not get the money.

Looking after ourselves can be fun. Whatever your passion is, bring it out and put it to work for yourself. It's the only way to survive in this crazy world. Stay focused.

Do not listen to the detractors. (If you have a lot of detractors around you, do not tell them what you are doing.) Listen to yourself and move forward.

Remember, there is no future in the past. We can learn from the past, but don't live there.

74

FREEDOM IS…
Zest For Your Life

Now go for what you truly want. Live your life to the fullest. Have fun and keep it real and legal. No pie in the sky stuff. Be who you are, a decent person, have everything that you want and give back to your community. Choose to step up into your Land of Paradise.

Since there are no guarantees in life, we have to do the best we can for ourselves and other people. So put your thinking caps on and get your life back on the track.

We can help each other do this. All you have to do is ask and you shall receive. Let's all get busy and take over our lives. One by one we can help each other to live their dreams.

I know it works because I have done it before and am doing it again. The Law of Attraction happens over and over.

THIS BOOK...

FREEDOM IS...does not mean we put up with home-grown or foreign killers, rapists, drug czars and addicts, drunk drivers (my daughter and her friend were almost killed by a drunk driver) corporate thugs (home-grown or international), harassers of any kind, anywhere on the planet. These types of people take other peoples freedoms away.

Yes, most people are free to make their own choices. Our laws take care of those who try to take our freedoms away. They lose their freedoms when they take other people's freedoms away. (This is freedom to love and live their lives in peace.)

People cannot do anything without freedom. I have always believed that people's freedoms, here in America and around the world. People choose different kinds of freedoms for themselves. This is why I was given the opportunity to write this book/journal.

There is nothing on the planet like freedom. People all over the world fight for freedom.

FREEDOM IS...what I make it.

FREEDOM IS...what you make it. Freedom makes it possible for me and you to live our lives and to achieve and live our dreams and to give back.

Most people love freedom. Stand up and cheer for yourself and for your freedoms. Freedom gives us, me and you, creativity, knowledge, goals, travel. People who stay home and cannot travel can also help by giving back by helping others. We all have the ability to express ourselves in many positive ways.

People can also object to the negative points in their lives. They can vote people out, not deal with people they do not like. Cut all the extra negative things. (credit cards, bad relationships, bad jobs.) Sometimes we have to earn our freedoms.

Taking freedom for granted is a huge mistake because without taking care of our freedoms, over time we could lose them. Nurturing, protecting and loving freedom is paramount to a happy life. Without freedom, we could not walk across the street without being stopped and asked where we are going. Without freedom, we could not travel from state to state. Without freedom, we could not travel from country to country. Freedom is…independence.

America and its citizens and future citizens are standing tall. We have survived a lot in the last 232 years and will continue to do so.

We are not perfect. No nation is. We learn from our mistakes, then make changes to do it better. The United States is a big, wide, wonderful country. Forty-eight states are connected to each other, with Alaska off Canada and Hawaii in the Pacific Ocean. All the states are different. The personalities of the people of America, with their diverse ethnic backgrounds, different heights, different shapes, different colors, different locations, different religions, different music, different languages, different amusements, different climates. This is what makes America great!

FREEDOM IS…for you and for me. Freedom gives us opportunity.

FREEDOM IS…We would not have come together if I were not free to think about my freedoms, write my freedoms, and have Trafford Publishing put my words in print for this book/journal. In this big, wide, wonderful world, there is nothing like freedom. When you live in freedom, your spirit soars just like an eagle. The American eagle is America's national bird. I can understand why. To soar like an eagle, it makes a person feel a hundred feet tall or a million feet tall, or any number in between. Without freedom, I could not have written this book/journal and had it published. It's just that simple.

Now, let's get to the freedoms, starting with mine. I have categorized my freedoms according to the types of freedoms. All my freedoms listed pertain to how I live my life everyday.

FREEDOM IS…
USA

FREEDOM IS…ABSOLUTE
FREEDOM IS…A BALANCING ACT
FREEDOM IS…OUR GIFT TO THE WORLD
FREEDOM IS…A TREASURE
FREEDOM IS…A TREAT
FREEDOM IS…AMERICAN
FREEDOM IS…AVAILABLE – but it takes time for many to be free.
FREEDOM IS…ADHERING TO FREEDOM
FREEDOM IS…AFFORDABLE
FREEDOM IS…ALMOST HEAVEN
FREEDOM IS…A RIGHT OF PASSAGE
FREEDOM IS…A DAYDREAM FOR MANY
FREEDOM IS…ANTICIPATED BY MANY
FREEDOM IS…A GREAT GIFT
FREEDOM IS…ASTRONOMICAL
FREEDOM IS…AUTOMATIC IN SOME COUNTRIES
FREEDOM IS…BASIC
FREEDOM IS…BENEFICIAL TO EVERYONE
FREEDOM IS…BETTER THAN THE ALTERNATIVE
FREEDOM IS…BELOVED
FREEDOM IS…BIG
FREEDOM IS…BOUNDLESS

FREEDOM IS...CLEAR
FREEDOM IS...CERTAIN
FREEDOM IS...CLASSIC
FREEDOM IS...CONTAGIOUS

FREEDOM IS...COSTLY, but without freedom, it's costlier!
FREEDOM IS...CRITICAL
FREEDOM IS...CIVIL RIGHTS
FREEDOM IS...CREATING HEROES
FREEDOM IS...CLUNG TO BY PEOPLE WORLDWIDE
FREEDOM IS...CONSTANT
FREEDOM IS...COMING TO MANY PEOPLE
FREEDOM IS...DEMONSTRATED
FREEDOM IS...DISCOVERING
FREEDOM IS...ENDLESS
FREEDOM IS...EVERYONE'S CHOICE
FREEDOM IS...ETERNAL
FREEDOM IS...KNOWING THAT EVERY STATE IS DIFFERENT.
                    (but all the states are connected by freedom.)
FREEDOM IS...EVERYONE'S DESIRE
FREEDOM IS...EFFECTIVE
FREEDOM IS...ENDORSED
FREEDOM IS...EARNED BY BIRTHRIGHT OR FOUGHT FOR
FREEDOM IS...ENTICING
FREEDOM IS...EVERLASTING
FREEDOM IS...EXPENSIVE
FREEDOM IS...ENDLESS (when it's nurtured)
FREEDOM IS...ENVIABLE
FREEDOM IS...FOR THE TAKING
FREEDOM IS...FOR ALL TO ENJOY
FREEDOM IS...FOREVER (when it's safe-guarded)
FREEDOM IS...FORSEEN BY THE MASSES
FREEDOM IS...FOR THE AGES
FREEDOM IS...A FACT OF LIFE
FREEDOM IS...FUNDAMENTAL
FREEDOM IS...FIRST
FREEDOM IS...FLOURISHING

FREEDOM IS...FOR EVERYONE
FREEDOM IS...GIVING PEACE A CHANCE
FREEDOM IS...GOLDEN
FREEDOM IS...GROWING
FREEDOM IS...GRAPHIC
FREEDOM IS...HONOR
FREEDOM IS...HOMELAND SECURITY
FREEDOM IS...HIGHLY RECOMMENDED
FREEDOM IS...HOPE
FREEDOM IS...HERE
FREEDOM IS...IDEALISTIC
FREEDOM IS...IMMEDIATE
FREEDOM IS...IMPERSTIVE
FREEDOM IS...IMPRESSIVE
FREEDOM IS...INDISPUTABLE
FREEDOM IS...WHAT IT IS!
FREEDOM IS...INDESTRUCTIBLE
FREEDOM IS...INDIVISABLE
FREEDOM IS...INSCRUTABLE
FREEDOM IS...A JOINT EFFORT
FREEDOM IS...JUSTICE
FREEDOM IS...JUSTIFIED
FREEDOM IS...KING
FREEDOM IS...KNOWN TO MANY PEOPLE

FREEDOM IS...LIKE AN EAGLE
FREEDOM IS...LIBERTY
FREEDOM IS...LEARNING THE RULES
FREEDOM IS...LAWS OF THE LAND
FREEDOM IS...LEGAL
FREEDOM IS...LIFE AND DEATH
FREEDOM IS...LONG-STANDING
FREEDOM IS...LONGED FOR BY MANY, WORLDWIDE
FREEDOM IS...MAGIC
FREEDOM IS...MESMERIZING
FREEDOM IS...MANY THINGS TO MANY PEOPLE
FREEDOM IS...MONUMENTAL

FREEDOM IS...MOST IMPORTANT
FREEDOM IS...NATURAL ORDER
FREEDOM IS...OBVIOUS
FREEDOM IS...NEVER –ENDING (when it's nurtured)
FREEDOM IS...NO BOUNDRIES (within reason)
FREEDOM IS...NECESSARY FOR ALL
FREEDOM IS...NEEDED BY MANY, WORLDWIDE
FREEDOM IS...NEVER TAKING FREEDOM FOR GRANTED
FREEDOM IS...NON-NEGOTIABLE

FREEDOM IS...NORMAL
FREEDOM IS...9-1-1 ONWARD
FREEDOM IS...NO ABUSE FROM ANYONE
FREEDOM IS...NOT TAKING OTHER PEOPLES FREEDOM
          AWAY
FREEDOM IS...OBSERVED BY MILLIONS
FREEDOM IS...ON-GOING
FREEDOM IS...OPEN FOR ALMOST ALL PEOPLE
FREEDOM IS...OUTSTANDING
FREEDOM IS...PRICELESS
FREEDOM IS...THE PURSUIT OF HAPPINESS
FREEDOM IS...PATRIOTIC
FREEDOM IS...PERCEIVED
FREEDOM IS...PICTURED
FREEDOM IS...PLENTIFUL
FREEDOM IS...PRAYED FOR WORLDWIDE
FREEDOM IS...PROMISED TO MANY WORLDWIDE
FREEDOM IS...PRINCIPLED
FREEDOM IS...PURE GUTS
FREEDOM IS...QUIETLY OBSERVED
FREEDOM IS...QUESTIONED AND ANSWERED

FREEDOM IS...QUINTESSENTIAL
FREEDOM IS...REALIST
FREEDOM IS...REASON
FREEDOM IS...REINFORCING
FREEDOM IS...REAL

FREEDOM IS...RIGHT
FREEDOM IS...SACRIFICE
FREEDOM IS...SACRED
FREEDOM IS...SCARCE IN SOME PLACES
FREEDOM IS...SHINING
FREEDOM IS...SOARING LIKE AN EAGLE
FREEDOM IS...SPECIAL
FREEDOM IS...SYMBOLIC
FREEDOM IS...SILENT
FREEDOM IS...SHARED BY MILLIONS
FREEDOM IS...TO DIE FOR
FREEDOM IS...TAKING ACTION
FREEDOM IS...THE ANCHOR
FREEDOM IS...TEAMWORK
FREEDOM IS...TEACHABLE
FREEDOM IS...TRUE GRIT
FREEDOM IS...TIMELESS

FREEDOM IS...THE SKY
FREEDOM IS...THERE FOR THE TAKING
FREEDOM IS...TOUGH
FREEDOM IS...THE BEST OF EVERYTHING
FREEDOM IS...TRADITION
FREEDOM IS...TO BE ENJOYED
FREEDOM IS...THE AMERICAN DREAM
FREEDOM IS...TENACITY
FREEDOM IS...THE OPENING ACT
FREEDOM IS...TRAVELING FREELY AROUND AMERICA
FREEDOM IS...TRAVELING FREELY WORLDWIDE
FREEDOM IS...UNSINKABLE
FREEDOM IS...UNDER GOD FOR ALL
FREEDOM IS...UNSPOKEN
FREEDOM IS...UNWAVERING
FREEDOM IS...VALUED
FREEDOM IS...VICTORY
FREEDOM IS...VITAL
FREEDOM IS...WHAT MATTERS

FREEDOM IS…WORTH IT
FREEDOM IS…WANTED BY ALL
FREEDOM IS…WHY PEOPLE MOVE TO AMERICA

FREEDOM IS…WELCOMED BY MANY PEOPLE WORLDWIDE
FREEDOM IS…ZEALOUS
FREEDOM IS…ZIPPING ALONG

76

FREEDOM IS…
Personal

FREEDOM IS…MY AMERICAN DREAM
FREEDOM IS…A BLESSING
FREEDOM IS…A BODY WRAP (a beautiful thing)
FREEDOM IS…ABUNDANCE AND GROWTH
FREEDOM IS…AFFIRMATIVE
FREEDOM IS…A GIFT FROM GOD
FREEDOM IS…AGREEING TO DISAGREE
FREEDOM IS…ALMOST PERFECT
FREEDOM IS…AMBITION
FREEDOM IS…ATTITUDE, NOT ALTITUDE
FREEDOM IS…A WISE CHOICE (getting a divorce)
FREEDOM IS…A LEARNING EXPERIENCE
FREEDOM IS…ADMITTING MY MISTAKES
FREEDOM IS…ACQUIRED BY WRITING FREEDOM IS…LOVING
            MYSELF AND OTHERS AND LIFE
FREEDOM IS…A LAS VEGAS BUFFET
FREEDOM IS…A WILL OF MY OWN
FREEDOM IS…BEAUTIFUL
FREEDOM IS…BECOMING TO ME
FREEDOM IS…BELIEVING IN IT
FREEDOM IS…A BEAUTIFUL BOUQUET
FREEDOM IS…ACCEPTING LIFE'S TESTS WITH A SMILE

FREEDOM IS...ACCESS
FREEDOM IS...ACCEPTING ADVICE
FREEDOM IS...ADAPTABILITY
FREEDOM IS...ADVANCING FORWARD
FREEDOM IS...A WEEKLY SPA TREATMENT
FREEDOM IS...BOUNCING BACK AFTER TURMOIL
FREEDOM IS...BEING FREE
FREEDOM IS...BELIEVING IN ME
FREEDOM IS...BEING GOOD TO MYSELF
FREEDOM IS...BEING TRUE TO MYSELF
FREEDOM IS...BEING ALONE WHEN I WANT TO BE ALONE
FREEDOM IS...BEING MY OWN BOSS
FREEDOM IS...BEING HEALTHY AND HAPPY
FREEDOM IS...BEING ME, MYSELF AND I

FREEDOM IS...BEING PERSISTENT
FREEDOM IS...BEING IN CONTROL OF MY PART OF THE
          WORLD
FREEDOM IS...BUYING WHAT I WANT
FREEDOM IS...BLOWING MY OWN HORN
FREEDOM IS...BEING KIND TO OTHERS
FREEDOM IS...BEING GENEROUS WITH MY TIME
FREEDOM IS...BEING GOOFY AT TIMES
FREEDOM IS...BETTER CHOICES
FREEDOM IS...CHALLENGING MYSELF
FREEDOM IS...MY FAVORITE CANDY
FREEDOM IS...CLIMBING MY MOUNTAINS
FREEDOM IS...CONFIDENCE GALORE
FREEDOM IS...CONGRATULATING MYSELF
FREEDOM IS...CONSCIOUS EFFORT
FREEDOM IS...COUNTRY MUSIC
FREEDOM IS...COURAGE
FREEDOM IS...CREATING WHAT I WANT
FREEDOM IS...COUNTRY LINE DANCING
FREEDOM IS...DANCING DOWN BROADWAY
FREEDOM IS...CHOOSING THE PEOPLE I WANT IN MY LIFE
FREEDOM IS...CHANGING MYSELF

FREEDOM IS...CHOOSING GOOD OVER EVIL
FREEDOM IS...DOING MY PERSONAL BEST
FREEDOM IS...DREAMING MY FUTURE
FREEDOM IS...DANCING TO THE OLDIES
FREEDOM IS...DANCING ALL NIGHT
FREEDOM IS...DEVELOPED
FREEDOM IS...DEALING ONLY WITH HONEST PEOPLE
FREEDOM IS...DIGNITY AND SELF-RESPECT
FREEDOM IS...DATING KIND PEOPLE
FREEDOM IS...DEALING OR NOT DEALING
FREEDOM IS...DARING TO DREAM
FREEDOM IS...DREAMING AS BIG AS THE SKY
FREEDOM IS...DISCOVERING MY TRUE SELF
FREEDOM IS...DISCOVERING MY STRENGTHS AND WEAKNESSES
FREEDOM IS...DOING THE RIGHT THING (even if it is not popular)
FREEDOM IS...DISAGREEING WITH A SMILE
FREEDOM IS...DARING TO TRY
FREEDOM IS...DOING THE 21 DAY PROGRAM (24/7)
FREEDOM IS...EARNED
FREEDOM IS...ENJOYING FOOD
FREEDOM IS...ENJOYING MYSELF AT WORK OR PLAY
FREEDOM IS...ENJOYING OTHERS AT WORK OR PLAY

FREEDOM IS...EMAILING
FREEDOM IS...EDUCATION
FREEDOM IS...EMPOWERING
FREEDOM IS...EQUALITY
FREEDOM IS...EXERCISING
FREEDOM IS...EYE-OPENING
FREEDOM IS...EXPLORING
FREEDOM IS...ENTREPRENURSHIP
FREEDOM IS...EVERYONE'S DREAM
FREEDOM IS...EMBRACING LIFE
FREEDOM IS...EVER-CHANGING
FREEDOM IS...EVERYTHING

FREEDOM IS...EXPERTISE
FREEDOM IS...FESTIVE
FREEDOM IS...EATING BROCCOLI
FREEDOM IS...EATING FUNNEL CAKES
FREEDOM IS...FAITH
FREEDOM IS...FAME (doing things for other people)
FREEDOM IS...FINDING TRUE FRIENDS
FREEDOM IS...A FIRE IN MY HEART
FREEDOM IS...FIRST (without it there is no second, third, fourth, fifth, etc.)
FREEDOM IS...FOREMOST

FREEDOM IS...FRIENDSHIPS
FREEDOM IS...FREE THINKING
FREEDOM IS...FENG SHEI
FREEDOM IS...FUN AND GAMES
FREEDOM IS...A FULL TANK OF GAS
FREEDOM IS...FAIRWAYS AND GREENS
FREEDOM IS...FOR ME
FREEDOM IS...GIVING HUGS
FREEDOM IS...GOODNESS IN MY HEART
FREEDOM IS...GRILLING FOOD
FREEDOM IS...GIVING ADVICE
FREEDOM IS...GOLFING
FREEDOM IS...GOD GIVEN
FREEDOM IS...GOD'S PROTECTION
FREEDOM IS...GETTING MY WAY (tactfully)
FREEDOM IS...GOING TO CHURCH
FREEDOM IS...GRACE UNDER FIRE
FREEDOM IS...GETTING A WEEKLY PEDICURE
FREEDOM IS...GOING ANYWHERE AT ANYTIME
FREEDOM IS...GUIDING MY CHILDREN
FREEDOM IS...HAVING SCRUPPLES

FREEDOM IS...HAVING CONTROL OF MY SITUATION IN MY PART OF THE WORLD
FREEDOM IS...HANGING IN THERE

FREEDOM IS...HANDLING PROBLEMS HEAD-ON
FREEDOM IS...HEALTHY SELF AND LIFE
FREEDOM IS...HELPING CHILDREN
FREEDOM IS...HEREDITRY
FREEDOM IS...I CAN DO ANYTHING
FREEDOM IS...IMAGINARY
FREEDOM IS...INDEPENDENT
FREEDOM IS...INTREGITY
FREEDOM IS...INVESTING IN ME
FREEDOM IS...INDIVIDUAL
FREEDOM IS...I RULE MY OWN WORLD
FREEDOM IS...MY INNER CHILD LOOSE AT DISNEY WORLD
FREEDOM IS...ICE CREAM YEAR ROUND (what fun!)
FREEDOM IS...JAMMING IN NEW ORLEANS (this wonderful city
        and surrounding states Alabama and Mississippi)
FREEDOM IS...JERSEY SHORE SALT WATER TAFFY
FREEDOM IS...JUST BEING ME
FREEDOM IS...JUMPING ROPE
FREEDOM IS...JOINING OR NOT JOINING
FREEDOM IS...KEY TO ANYTHING (LEGAL) I CHOSE TO DO

FREEDOM IS...JOKING AROUND
FREEDOM IS...KNOWLEDGE
FREEDOM IS...KNOWING GOD
FREEDOM IS...KNOWING WHAT FREEDOM REALLY MEANS
FREEDOM IS...KNOWING MYSELF
FREEDOM IS...KNOWING WHAT I REALLY WANT
FREEDOM IS...KEEPING MY SPIRITS UP
FREEDOM IS...KNOWING WHAT LIFE REALLY MEANS
FREEDOM IS...KNOWING I REALLY, REALLY LIKE MYSELF
FREEDOM IS...KNOWING THAT I AM LOVED AND LIKED
FREEDOM IS...KNOWING WHAT TO DO AND WHEN TO DO
        IT
FREEDOM IS...LET GO AND LET GOD
FREEDOM IS...LIVING MY FREEDOMS
FREEDOM IS...LIVING THE TEN COMMANDMENTS
FREEDOM IS...LISTENING TO CNN

FREEDOM IS...LIVING LIFE
FREEDOM IS...LIVING IN HARMONY
FREEDOM IS...LIVING EACH DAY TO THE FULLEST
FREEDOM IS...LIVING MY DREAMS
FREEDOM IS...LIVING FREE
FREEDOM IS...LIVING ACCORDING TO WHAT I BELIEVE

FREEDOM IS...LIVING THROUGH HELL
FREEDOM IS...LEARNING TO TRUST AGAIN
FREEDOM IS...LEARNING FROM MY MISTAKES
FREEDOM IS...LEAVING A LEGACY AFTER I AM GONE
FREEDOM IS...LIVING WITHOUT FEAR
FREEDOM IS...LOOKING FORWARD NOT BEHIND
FREEDOM IS...LIVING WHERE MY HEART IS
FREEDOM IS...LOOKING AT THE WONDERS AROUND ME
FREEDOM IS...LIVING BY THE RULES
FREEDOM IS...LONGEVITY
FREEDOM IS...LOTS OF KUDOS
FREEDOM IS...LOVE
FREEDOM IS...LOOKING BEYOND MYSELF
FREEDOM IS...LIVING MY BEST LIFE
FREEDOM IS...LOVING MY LIFE
FREEDOM IS...LIVING ON MY OWN TERMS
FREEDOM IS...LOYALTY TO MYSELF, MY FAMILY, MY FRIENDS,
            MY COUNTRY
FREEDOM IS...MONEY (OBTAINED LEGALLY)
FREEDOM IS...MINE
FREEDOM IS...MOBILITY
FREEDOM IS...MY OWN TIME

FREEDOM IS...BARRIERS GONE (ALWAYS LEGAL)
FREEDOM IS...A NON-JUDGMENTAL ATTITUDE
FREEDOM IS...OBEYING LAWS OF AMERICA AND OTHER
            COUNTRIES
FREEDOM IS...OWNING MY LIFE
FREEDOM IS...ONE DAY AT A TIME
FREEDOM IS...OPENING UP TO LIFE'S GIFTS

FREEDOM IS...AN OPEN HEART
FREEDOM IS...PARTY HARDY
FREEDOM IS...PERSONAL
FREEDOM IS...PHILLY STEAKS AND SOFT PRETZELS
FREEDOM IS...RITA'S WATER ICE
FREEDOM IS...PARTICIPATION
FREEDOM IS...PRIDE IN MYSELF AND MY COUNTRY
FREEDOM IS...PRIVATE TIMES
FREEDOM IS...PUTTING ALL THE LIGHTS ON IN THE MIDDLE
            OF THE NIGHT
FREEDOM IS...PICKING MY BATTLES
FREEDOM IS...PUBLIC SPEAKING
FREEDOM IS...PROFITABLE
FREEDOM IS...PLAYING MY OWN TUNE
FREEDOM IS...PASSING ALL GOD'S TESTS
FREEDOM IS...PAMPERING MYSELF AND OTHERS

FREEDOM IS...PEACEFUL
FREEDOM IS...PRIORTIES
FREEDOM IS...PLAYING GOLF WORLDWIDE
FREEDOM IS...PICTURING MY FUTURE
FREEDOM IS...PRECIOUS
FREEDOM IS...RECOVERING
FREEDOM IS...RESPECTING OTHERS
FREEDOM IS...REACHABLE
FREEDOM IS...RESPECTING MYSELF
FREEDOM IS...REALLY SMELLING THE ROSES
FREEDOM IS...REALIZING HOW LUCKY I AM
FREEDOM IS...REJUVENATING
FREEDOM IS...RELEASING MYSELF
FREEDOM IS...RE-INVENTING MYSELF
FREEDOM IS...RELAXING ON THE WEEKEND
FREEDOM IS...RENTING A LIMO WHEN NEEDED
FREEDOM IS...ROCK AND ROLL MUSIC AND DANCING
FREEDOM IS...SERVICE TO OTHERS
FREEDOM IS...SHARING MY LIFE
FREEDOM IS...SIGNING

FREEDOM IS…SHOPPING
FREEDOM IS…SHARING
FREEDOM IS…SPEAKING MY MIND (loud and clear)

FREEDOM IS…SINGING OFF KEY
FREEDOM IS…SNACKS ANYTIME
FREEDOM IS…SELF WORTH
FREEDOM IS…SITTING UNDER A WILLOW TREE ON A
          SUMMER DAY
FREEDOM IS…STEPPING UP TO THE PLATE
FREEDOM IS…STANDING UP FOR WHAT I BELIEVE
FREEDOM IS…STANDING UP FOR MYSELF
FREEDOM IS…SWINGING TO THE OLDIES
FREEDOM IS…SOUL SEARCHING
FREEDOM IS…SPIRITUAL
FREEDOM IS…STANDING UP FOR AMERICA
FREEDOM IS…STYLE
FREEDOM IS…SUCCEEDING
FREEDOM IS…SURPRISING OTHERS (beneficial)
FREEDOM IS…SURVIVING THE BAD STUFF
FREEDOM IS…SAYING NOTHING AT ALL
FREEDOM IS…STANDING MY GROUND
FREEDOM IS…STREET SMARTS
FREEDOM IS…SPONSORING PGA EVENTS
FREEDOM IS…TRUSTING MYSELF
FREEDOM IS…THINKING MY OWN THOUGHTS

FREEDOM IS…TAKING RISKS
FREEDOM IS…USING MY HEAD
FREEDOM IS…UNCANNY VISION FROM GOD
FREEDOM IS…WELCOMED
FREEDOM IS…WHAT I AM AND DO
FREEDOM IS…WORKING ON MYSELF
FREEDOM IS…WHAT DREAMS ARE MADE OF
FREEDOM IS…WHAT I MAKE IT
FREEDOM IS…WALKING OUT OF A MAZE
FREEDOM IS…WALKING 1 MILE (four times a week)

FREEDOM IS...WRITING FREEDOM IS...a Book/Journal with a
                Twist!
FREEDOM IS...YEARNED FOR BY MANY WORLDWIDE
FREEDOM IS...ZEST FOR LIFE

77

FREEDOM IS…
Feelings

FREEDOM IS…AFFECTION
FREEDOM IS…ALIVE AND WELL
FREEDOM IS…ALL AROUND ME
FREEDOM IS…AMAZING
FREEDOM IS…AN AWAKENING
FREEDOM IS…AGREEING TO DISAGREE
FREEDOM IS…A BLAST (fun)
FREEDOM IS…ACCELERATING
FREEDOM IS…ACCEPTANCE
FREEDOM IS…A STATE OF MIND
FREEDOM IS…ASTONISHING
FREEDOM IS…ATTRACTIVE
FREEDOM IS…ABIDING LOVE
FREEDOM IS…A BREATH OF FRESH AIR
FREEDOM IS…BIGGER THAN LIFE
FREEDOM IS…BEING POSITIVE
FREEDOM IS…BEING FEARLESS
FREEDOM IS…BREATH-TAKING
FREEDOM IS…BECOMING
FREEDOM IS…BELIEVING IN YOURSELF
FREEDOM IS…BOUNDLESS
FREEDOM IS…CAPTIVATING

FREEDOM IS...CARING
FREEDOM IS...CHARACTER
FREEDOM IS...CONNECTED
FREEDOM IS...CLEAR
FREEDOM IS...COMFORTING MYSELF
FREEDOM IS...CONTENTMENT
FREEDOM IS...COOL
FREEDOM IS...COUNTING MY BLESSING
FREEDOM IS...DELIGHTFUL
FREEDOM IS...DESIRED
FREEDOM IS...DETERMINATION
FREEDOM IS...ELECTRIC
FREEDOM IS...ENERGY
FREEDOM IS...EMOTIONAL
FREEDOM IS...ENDEARING
FREEDOM IS...ENTHUSIASTISM
FREEDOM IS...EXPRESSIVE
FREEDOM IS...EXTRAORDINARY
FREEDOM IS...EXHILARATING
FREEDOM IS...EXCITING
FREEDOM IS...FEELING GREAT
FREEDOM IS...FANTASTIC
FREEDOM IS...FEARLESS
FREEDOM IS...FEELING FEARLESS
FREEDOM IS...FIRE IN MY HEART
FREEDOM IS...GOOD SENSE
FREEDOM IS...GOD IS NOT FINISHED WITH ME YET!
FREEDOM IS...GREAT
FREEDOM IS...GIVING BACK, BIG TIME
FREEDOM IS...HAVING A BIG HEART
FREEDOM IS...HARMONY
FREEDOM IS...HEARTFELT
FREEDOM IS...HEARING A DIFFERENT DRUMMER
FREEDOM IS...HEALING
FREEDOM IS...HUMOR
FREEDOM IS...HUMAN
FREEDOM IS...HUMBLING

FREEDOM IS...INSIDE/OUTSIDE
FREEDOM IS...INSTINCTIVE
FREEDOM IS...INVITING
FREEDOM IS...INTENSE
FREEDOM IS...KINDNESS
FREEDOM IS...KNOWING JOY
FREEDOM IS...KEEP ON, KEEPING ON
FREEDOM IS...KINSHIP
FREEDOM IS...KNOWING MOM'S SPIRIT IS ALWAYS WITH ME
      (Keeping me grounded)
FREEDOM IS...LETTING MY HEART SING
FREEDOM IS...LAUGHING THROUGH TEARS
FREEDOM IS...LAUGHING OUT LOUD
FREEDOM IS...LEARNING FROM MY MISTAKES
FREEDOM IS...LIVING FREE
FREEDOM IS...MASTERFUL
FREEDOM IS...NEVER GIVING UP (even when I want to)
FREEDOM IS...PASSIONATE
FREEDOM IS...POWERFUL
FREEDOM IS...PARAMOUNT
FREEDOM IS...REFRESHING
FREEDOM IS...ROCK AND ROLL MUSIC, COUNTRY MUSIC
FREEDOM IS...REMEMBERING FUN TIMES
FREEDOM IS...SEEING GOD'S BLESSINGS
FREEDOM IS...SINGING IN THE RAIN
FREEDOM IS...SATISFACTION
FREEDOM IS...SENSING MY BROTHER GEORGE'S SPIRIT IS
      ALWAYS WITH ME (and hugging me when I need it)
FREEDOM IS...STRENGTH
FREEDOM IS...SUBLIME
FREEDOM IS...STREET SMART MENTALITY
FREEDOM IS...THRILLING
FREEDOM IS...UNAFRAID
FREEDOM IS...UPLIFTING
FREEDOM IS...UNDERSTANDING DIFFERENT TYPES OF PAIN
FREEDOM IS...WONDERFUL
FREEDOM IS...WHISTLING DOWN THE LANE

FREEDOM IS…
What I Like To Do

FREEDOM IS…ACTING SILLY
FREEDOM IS…A MERRY-GO-ROUND RIDE
FREEDOM IS…A HAMMOCK
FREEDOM IS…A TRIP TO THE ZOO
FREEDOM IS…THE BEACH
FREEDOM IS…BEING FUNNY
FREEDOM IS…LOTS OF CANDY
FREEDOM IS…CHERISHING LIFE AND PEOPLE
FREEDOM IS…COMMUNICATION
FREEDOM IS…CAREFREE DAYS
FREEDOM IS…DOUBLE DUTCH JUMP ROPE
FREEDOM IS…DRIVING THE FREEWAYS
FREEDOM IS…EATING WHAT I WANT (within reason)
FREEDOM IS…ENJOYING WHAT IS AROUND ME
FREEDOM IS…EXPERIENCING MY LIFE
FREEDOM IS…FOOD SHOPPING AT MIDNIGHT
FREEDOM IS…GOLFING
FREEDOM IS…GOING TO A SPA
FREEDOM IS…HELPING OTHER PEOPLE
FREEDOM IS…HONESTY
FREEDOM IS…HUMMING A TUNE
FREEDOM IS…KELLOGG'S FROOT LOOPS

FREEDOM IS...KASHI'S HEART TO HEART
FREEDOM IS...LOTS OF ICE CREAM
FREEDOM IS...LIVING IN THE PRESENT
FREEDOM IS...LOVE WHAT I DO
FREEDOM IS...LOVE...HAVING FUN, LIVING LIFE TO THE
FULLEST
FREEDOM IS...LAZY DAYS (every once in awhile)
FREEDOM IS...MANDARIN ORANGES
FREEDOM IS...NASCAR RACING
FREEDOM IS...PEACE AND QUIET
FREEDOM IS...RAIN
FREEDOM IS...ROCK AND ROLL MUSIC
FREEDOM IS...SURVIVING WHATEVER I NEED TO SURVIVE
FREEDOM IS...SELF-DEFENSE
FREEDOM IS...PEAKING AT SEMINARS
FREEDOM IS...SPEAKING AT UNIVERSITY'S AND COLLEGES
FREEDOM IS...STRAIGHT TALK
FREEDOM IS...SIMPLE PLEASURES
FREEDOM IS...STAYING FOCUSED ON WHAT IS REALLY
IMPORTANT
FREEDOM IS...TRUTH
FREEDOM IS...TAKING A DEEP BREATH
FREEDOM IS...24-HOUR MOVIE MARATHONS
FREEDOM IS...HOT GREEN TEA AND CINNAMON BUNS
FREEDOM IS...THROWING OUT, GIVING AWAY OR SELLING
WHAT IS NOT USED
FREEDOM IS...WHITE PIZZA
FREEDOM IS...WATCHING WILD HORSES RUN IN THE
WESTERN STATES
FREEDOM IS...WISHING ON A STAR

FREEDOM IS...
Travel

FREEDOM IS...ADVENTURE

FREEDOM IS...ROAD TRIPS WORLDWIDE

FREEDOM IS...ARCHEOLOGICAL SITE VACATIONS WORLDWIDE

FREEDOM IS...A LAS VEGAS SUNSET (It's a Beautiful Thing)

FREEDOM IS...A KEY WEST SUNSET (It's a Beautiful Thing)

FREEDOM IS...A SUNRISE AT WONDERFUL GLADSTONES-ON-THE-BEACH, MALIBU, CALIFORNIA (it's a beautiful thing)

FREEDOM IS...A SUNSET AT THE CASTAWAYS HILLTOP RESTAURANT – BURBANK, CALIFORNIA (sitting outside watching the twinkling stars above; twinkling lights below, so wonderfully peaceful, I wanted to sleep there all night.)

FREEDOM IS...A DISAPPEARING ACT...(when you have to get someone's attention or save your life.)

FREEDOM IS...BEACHES WORLDWIDE

FREEDOM IS...BEING GLOBAL

FREEDOM IS...BEAUTIFUL VIEWS AT PEPPERDINE UNIVERSITY, MALIBU, CALIFORNIA (bright blue ocean, lush green grass, white buildings, what a beautiful and peaceful site.)

FREEDOM IS...FOOTBALL GAMES AT NOTRE DAME UNIVERSITY, SOUTH BEND, INDIANA. (sat in the rain, snow, sleet and hail)

FREEDOM IS...CRUISING THE WORLD (Greek Isles, Hawaiian Islands, Caribbean Islands)

FREEDOM IS...CASINO COUPON BOOKS (fun, fun, fun)

FREEDOM IS...DANCING DOWN BROADWAY IN NEW YORK CITY

FREEDOM IS...DANCING DOWN THE LAS VEGAS STRIP

FREEDOM IS...HAWAII – FLOATING ON A RAFT IN A POOL

FREEDOM IS...NEW YORK CITY, TRUMP TOWER, EMPIRE STATE BUILDING, STATUE OF LIBERTY, THEATRES, ST. PATRICK'S CATHEDRAL, ROCKEFELLER CENTER

FREEDOM IS...BEAUTIFUL FLORIDA, HOLLYWOOD, FORT LAUDERDALE, ORLANDO, ST. AUGUSTINE, NAPLES, MARCO ISLAND, JACKSONVILLE, ST. PETERSBURG

FREEDOM IS...FLYING FOR A QUICK TRIP - PRIVATE PLANE

FREEDOM IS...CROSS-COUNTRY TRAIN RIDE (great people; beautiful America; what a great country)

FREEDOM IS...COLORADO – A MAJESTIC PICTURE POSTCARD STATE

FREEDOM IS...DISNEY WORLD AND DISNEY LAND VACATIONS (wearing Mickey ears at the park)

FREEDOM IS...SUMMER AND WINTER OLYMPICS

FREEDOM IS...THE GRAND CANYON

FREEDOM IS...OUR NATIONAL PARKS

FREEDOM IS...RINCON, PUERTO RICO (love this place)

FREEDOM IS...THE SOUTHWEST STATES (BIG SKY COUNTRY)

FREEDOM IS...LAS VEGAS, NV AND ORLANDO, FL (live where it is fun)

FREEDOM IS...THE TRADEWINDS

FREEDOM IS...BEING MOBILE

FREEDOM IS...THE TROPICS

FREEDOM IS...YEARLY TRIPS AROUND AMERICA

FREEDOM IS...
Goals

FREEDOM IS...ATTAINABLE

FREEDOM IS...A WEEKLY MASSAGE

FREEDOM IS...A HYBRID CAR

FREEDOM IS...ACCOMPLISHING MY GOALS

FREEDOM IS...A GOLF COURSE VIEW

FREEDOM IS...A-HOLE-IN-ONE

FREEDOM IS...A PRIVATE JET

FREEDOM IS...APPEARING ON ABC SOAP OPERAS (All My Children; One Life To Live: General Hospital)

FREEDOM IS...APPEARING on Rescue Me, Las Vegas, Desperate Housewives, Boston Legal, CSI (Las Vegas, Miami and New York), Law and Order SVU, The View, Shark, The Tonight Show, The Late Show with David Letterman, Jimmy Kimmel, GMA, Real Time with Bill Maher, Oprah, Today Show, GMA, The Early Show, Hardball, CNN, Fox, Larry King, The O'Reilly Factor, Nancy Grace, Glenn Beck, Radio Shows across the country.

FREEDOM IS...APPEARING ON THE OPRAH SHOW

FREEDOM IS...CHARITY EVENTS

FREEDOM IS...CREATING HEROES

FREEDOM IS...CREATING SPECIAL THINGS FOR ALL TO ENJOY

FREEDOM IS...CONTRIBUTING SOMETHING WORTHWHILE
        FOR THE AGES TO ENJOY
FREEDOM IS...DONATING TO CHARITIES
FREEDOM IS...EXPRESSING FREEDOM IS DIFFERENT WAYS
FREEDOM IS...FINDING PEACEFUL SOLUTIONS TO
        WORLDWIDE PROBLEMS
FREEDOM IS...HELPING PEOPLE DISCOVER THEIR FIELD OF
        DREAMS
FREEDOM IS...HELPING PEOPLE FOCUS ON THEIR FREEDOMS
        THROUGH THIS BOOK/JOURNAL

FREEDOM IS...HELPING PEOPLE FOCUS ON WHAT THEY
        REALLY WANT
FREEDOM IS...MOVING FORWARD
FREEDOM IS...OPRAH'S ANGEL NETWORK
FREEDOM IS...GIVING BACK TO AMERICA
FREEDOM IS...STAYING GOAL-ORIENTED
FREEDOM IS...HAPPENINGS IN DIFFERENT PLACES THAT I
        HAVE YET TO SEE
FREEDOM IS...HABITAT FOR HUMANITY (working with them)
FREEDOM IS...HOSTING MY RADIO SHOW (helping people live
        wonderful lives)
FREEDOM IS...NEW IDEAS, PLUS IDEALS
FREEDOM IS...INFINITE PROSPERITY FOR ALL FREEDOM
        LOVING PEOPLE
FREEDOM IS...PILATES, KICK-BOXING
FREEDOM IS...PUBLISHING MORE BOOKS (they are in the works)
FREEDOM IS...LEAVING MY MARK TO HELP OTHERS LEAVE
        THEIR MARK
FREEDOM IS...LEARY FIGHTFIGHTER'S FOUNDATION
FREEDOM IS...LIVING LIFE TO THE FULLEST
FREEDOM IS...LAND AND BUILDINGS FOR DIFFERENT
        VENTURES
FREEDOM IS...MAKING WISE DECISIONS
FREEDOM IS...TRAVELING THROUGHOUT AMERICA EACH
        YEAR
FREEDOM IS...RIVER BOATING AROUND THE WORLD

FREEDOM IS...SPA VACATIONS

FREEDOM IS...SEDONA, ARIZONA

FREEDOM IS...STARTING A FOUNDATION

FREEDOM IS...HELPING THE ASPCA WITH THE ANIMALS. (Just Love Dogs!)

FREEDOM IS...SAVING LIVES, ONE PERSON AT A TIME

FREEDOM IS...STAYING AT CASTLES IN IRELAND, ENGLAND, FRANCE, GERMANY, SPAIN

FREEDOM IS...STOPPING DOMESTIC VIOLENCE EVERYWHERE

FREEDOM IS...STOPPING HARASSMENT EVERYWHERE

FREEDOM IS...SPONSORING A TEAM

FREEDOM IS...TAHITI AND FIJI

FREEDOM IS...TRAVELING IN SPACE

FREEDOM IS...VACATIONING WORLDWIDE

FREEDOM IS...VOLUNTEERING

FREEDOM IS...OWNING VENDING MACHINES

FREEDOM IS...WORLD GOLF HALL OF FAME IN ST. AUGUSTINE, FLORIDA

FREEDOM IS...YEARLY TRIPS THROUGHOUT AMERICA (just love it!)

FREEDOM IS...WRITING A COLUMN IN ACROSS AMERICA NEWPAPERS

FREEDOM IS...WRITING AND HELPING PEOPLE ON MY FUN WEBSITE. www.kathywenselinternational.com

FREEDOM IS...WRITING A SITCON AND TV MOVIE OF THE WEEK, PLUS A MOTION PICTURE (about my brother George Wensel, one of the really good guys)

FREEDOM IS…
Letting Go Of

FREEDOM IS…BEEN THERE, DONE THAT, NOT AGAIN

FREEDOM IS…BREATHING WITHOUT FEAR

FREEDOM IS…ABUSIVE PEOPLE OUT OF MY LIFE

FREEDOM IS…A DIVORCE (one of the best things I ever did)

FREEDOM IS…ELIMINATING STRESS FOREVER

FREEDOM IS…FORGIVING, BUT NOT FORGETTING

FREEDOM IS…NO FRUSTRATION AT ALL

FREEDOM IS…IF IT'S NOT FUN (AND LEGAL) I'M NOT DOING IT!

FREEDOM IS…KEEP KICKING SATAN TO THE CURB

FREEDOM IS…OVERCOMING OBSTACLES

FREEDOM IS…NOT SWEATING THE SMALL STUFF OR THE BIG STUFF

FREEDOM IS…NO HARASSMENT IN THE WORKPLACE OR ANY OTHER PLACE (book in the works)

FREEDOM IS…LIVING WITHOUT THREATS

FREEDOM IS...
My Pet Peeves

FREEDOM IS...NO CLUELESS PERSON SHOULD HANDLE ANYTHING THAT DEALS WITH PEOPLE ANYPLACE, ANYWHERE, ANYTIME. (because, they just make people's lives miserable)

FREEDOM IS...NOT DEALING WITH ANY AIRHEADS

FREEDOM IS...NOT DEALING WITH ANY MORONS

FREEDOM IS...NOT DEALING WITH ANY IDIOTS

FREEDOM IS...NOT DEALING WITH ANY TRUTHFULLY CHALLENGED PEOPLE (a lie is a lie)

FREEDOM IS...NOT DEALING WITH ANY BACK STABBERS

FREEDOM IS...NOT DEALING WITH ANY BOZOS

FREEDOM IS...NOT DEALING WITH ANY DEWEEBS

FREEDOM IS...NOT DEALING WITH ANY DIRT BAGS

FREEDOM IS...NOT DEALING WITH ANY CREEPS

FREEDOM IS...NOT DEALING WITH ANY CRAP

FREEDOM IS...NOT DEALING WITH CONTROL FREAKS

FREEDOM IS...NOT DEALING WITH CELL PHONES WHERE CELL PHONES SHOULD NOT BE (movies, plays, church, restaurants)

FREEDOM IS...NOT DEALING WITH ANY DISHONEST PEOPLE

FREEDOM IS...NOT DEALING WITH ANY DISFUNCTIONAL ROADSHOWS

FREEDOM IS...NOT DEALING WITH ANY ETHICALLY CHALLENGED PEOPLE

FREEDOM IS...NOT DEALING WITH ANY JERKS

FREEDOM IS...NOT DEALING WITH ANY FAKES

FREEDOM IS...NOT DEALING WITH ANY HARASSERS, ANYWHERE, ANYTIME

FREEDOM IS...NOT DEALING WITH ANY LOONIES

FREEDOM IS...NOT DEALING WITH ANY MENTAL PIGMIES

FREEDOM IS...NOT DEALING WITH ANY CORPORATE THUGS

FREEDOM IS...NOT DEALING WITH INTEGRITY CHALLENGED PEOPLE

FREEDOM IS...NOT DEALING WITH MORALLY CHALLENGED PEOPLE

FREEDOM IS...NOT DEALING WITH ANY NUTCASES

FREEDOM IS...NOT DEALING WITH ANY PLASTIC PEOPLE

FREEDOM IS...NOT DEALING WITH PSYCHOS

FREEDOM IS...NOT DEALING WITH SNOOTY PEOPLE

FREEDOM IS...NOT DEALING WITH SOCIOPATHS

FREEDOM IS...NOT DEALING WITH SHALLOW PEOPLE

FREEDOM IS...NOT DEALING WITH OFF-THE-WALL WHACK-O'S

FREEDOM IS...NOT DEALING WITH ANY TWITS

FREEDOM IS...NOT DEALING WITH ANY WIMPS

FREEDOM IS...NOT DEALING WITH ANY TERRORISTS OF ANY KIND (home-grown or foreign)

FREEDOM IS...NOT DEALING WITH ANY FUNNY FARM CANDIDATES

FREEDOM IS...NOT DEALING WITH ANY SCUMBAGS

FREEDOM IS...NOT DEALING WITH ANY CRAZY'S ("When you see crazy coming, cross the street." Thank You, Oprah.)

FREEDOM IS...KNOWING THAT YOU CAN PICK YOUR FRIENDS, BUT YOU CAN'T PICK YOUR RELATIVES. REMEMBER, YOUR FRIENDS ARE GOD'S GIFTS TO YOU!

I have met these types of people throughout my life and choose not to deal with any of these types of people, ever again! They will drain and zap your energy and your spirit.

I know some people will say that from the above list there are not many good people left. Not true! There are millions of good people on the planet. Good people stand out. Just look around. You will see good people, everywhere!

Life is what I make it. Life is what you make it. Life is simple. We humans make life difficult. Get rid of all the unwanted things (sometimes people included) in your life. It's wonderful. You will feel so much lighter. The more simple your life is, the more you will enjoy your life. I know this because I am doing it myself. Almost everyone knows about the Ten Commandments. No matter what religion a person is, they know what is true. Passing all the tests that are given are easier when you make your life simple. Life is so complicated now for so many people, simplicity makes everything better.

As of July 4th, 2008, America turned 232 years old. How cool is that for all the citizens of America? Always be happy, healthy and live your dreams.

REMEMBER,
FREEDOM IS...

QUESTIONAIRE FOR WEBSITE

Since I have been through about of different things in my life, I can help a lot of people.

Since you have read the Book/Journal, I have a few questions for you. What are your freedoms?

Please let me know what you want me to talk about?

I look forward to working with you in different venues, such as: my Radio Show, Teleseminars, Joint Ventures, ebooks, speaking across the country and more to come.

Website: *www.kathywenslinternational.com*

www.mypowermall.com/mall/145863
This site helps the "Together We Can Change The World"
Just sit back, save gas and shop online!

FREEDOM IS...
Now It Is Up To You...People Worldwide

Now, it is your turn to write your freedoms. Have a great time writing your freedoms.

UNITED STATES
PRESIDENTIAL QUOTES

The quotes listed below are from dead U.S. President's. It is really amazing how most of the quotes fit what is going on in the world today. History certainly does repeat itself.

01. GEORGE WASHINGTON (1789-1797)

"I walk on untrodden ground. There is scarcely any part of my conduct which may not hereafter be drawn into precedent."

"To be prepared for war is one of the most effectual means of preserving peace."

"Government is not reason; it is not eloquence; it is force! Like fire, it is a dangerous servant and a fearful master."

"Few men have virtue to withstand the highest bidder."

"Liberty, when it begins to take root, is a plant of rapid growth."

"Government is not reason, it is not eloquence, it is force; like fire, a troublesome servant and a fearful master. Never for a moment should it be left to irresponsible action."

"To be prepared for War is one of the most effectual means of preserving peace."

"In a free and republican government, you cannot restrain the voice of the multitude."

"If the freedom of speech is taken away then dumb and silent we may be led, like sheep to the slaughter."

"Obey God, serve mankind, oppose tyranny."

"The best way to have peace is to always be prepared to find a way."

"Labor to keep alive in your breast that little spark of celestial fire called conscience."

"To err is natural; to rectify error is glory."

"True friendship is a plant of slow growth."

"To contract new debts is not the way to pay old ones."

"Associate with men of good quality if you esteem your own reputation, for it is better to be alone than in bad company."

"Be courteous to all, but intimate with few, and let those few be well tried before you give them your confidence."

"Few men have virtue to withstand the highest bidder."

"An army of asses led by a lion is better than an army of Lions led by an ass."

"I attribute my success in life to the moral, intellectual and physical education which I received from my mother."

"Let your heart feel for the affliction and distress of everyone."

"When we assumed the Soldier, we did not lay aside the Citizen."

"I hate deception, even where the imagination only is concerned."

"The opinion and advice of my friends I receive at all times as a proof of their friendship and am thankful when they are offered."

"Happiness and moral duty are inseparably connected."

"The marvel of all history is the patience with which men and women submit to burdens unnecessarily laid upon them by their government."

"Guard against the impostures of pretended patriotism."

"Observe good faith and justice toward all nations. Cultivate peace and harmony with all."

"Let us raise a standard to which the wise and honest can repair; the rest is in the hands of God."

"Truth will ultimately prevail where there is pains to bring it to light."

"I hope I shall possess firmness and virtue enough to maintain what I consider the most enviable of all titles; the character of an honest man."

"My first wish is to see this plague of mankind, war, banished from the earth."

"It is well, I die hard, but I am not afraid to go."

02. JOHN ADAMS (1797-1801)

"By my physical constitution, I am but an ordinary man. The times alone have destined me to fame – and even these have not been able to give me much."

"I always consider the settlement of America with reverence and wonder, as the opening of a grand scene and design in providence, for the illumination of the ignorant and the emancipation of the slavish part of mankind all over the earth."

"A pen is certainly an excellent instrument to fix a man's attention and to inflame his ambition."

"Arms in the hands of citizens may be used at individual discretion… in private self-defense."

"I pray Heaven to bestow the best of blessing on this house (the White House) and on all that shall hereafter inhabit it. May none but honest and wise men ever rule under this roof!"

"Let every sluice of knowledge be open and set a-flowing."

"All great changes are irksome to the human, especially those which are attended with great dangers and uncertain effects."

"The happiness of society as the end of government."

"Facts are stubborn things, and whatever may be our wishes, our inclinations, or the dictates of our passions, they cannot after the state of facts and evidence."

"Democracy…while it lasts is more bloody than either aristocracy or monarchy. Remember; democracy never lasts long. It soon wastes, exhausts, and murders itself. There is never a democracy that did not commit suicide."

"I must study politics and war that my sons may have liberty to study mathematics and philosophy."

"Let justice be done though the heavens should fall."

"Liberty cannot be preserved without a general knowledge among the people, who have…a right, an indisputable, unalienable, indefeasible, divine right to that most dreaded and envied kind of knowledge, I mean the characters and conduct of their rulers."

"It is weakness rather than wickedness which rendered men unfit to be trusted with unlimited power."

"If we do not lay out ourselves in the service of mankind whom should we serve?

"All the perplexities, confusion and distress in American arise, not from defects in their Constitution or Confederation, not from want of honor or virtue, so much as from the downright ignorance of the nature of coin, credit and circulation."

"When people talk of the freedom of writing, speaking or thinking I cannot choose but, laugh. No such thing ever existed. No such thing now exists: but I hope it will exist. But, it must be hundreds of years after you and I shall write and speak no more. (1st Vice-President of the United States and 2nd President of the United States)

"Property must be secured, or liberty cannot exist."

"Let us dare to read, think, speak and write."

"We should begin by setting conscience free."

"A government of laws, and not of men."

"I agree with you that in politics the middle way is none at all."

"Fear is the foundation of most governments."

"Facts are stubborn things; and whatever may be our wishes, our inclinations, or the dictates of our passions, they cannot alter the state of facts and evidence."

"For a nation to be free, it is only necessary that she wills it."

"Old minds are like old horses, you must exercise them if you wish to keep them in working order."

"Grief drives men to serious reflection, sharpens the understanding and softens the heart."

"Straight is the gate and narrow is the way that leads to liberty, and few nations, if any, have found it."

"Think of your forefathers! Think of your posterity."

"When people talk of the freedom of writing, speaking, or thinking, I cannot choose but laugh. No such thing ever existed. No such thing now exists; but I hope it will exist. But it must be hundreds of years after you and I shall write and speak no more. (from a letter to Thomas Jefferson, 1818)

"Genius is sorrow's child."

"A desire to be observed, considered, esteemed, praised, beloved, and admired by his fellows is one of the earliest as well as the keenest dispositions discovered in the heart of man."

"Be not intimidated...nor suffer yourselves to be wheedled out of your liberties by any pretense of politeness, delicacy, or decency. These, as they are often used, are but three different names for hypocrisy, chicanery and cowardice."

"Power always thinks it has a great soul and vast views beyond the comprehension of the weak."

"My country has contrived for me the most insignificant office that ever the invention of man contrived or his imagination conceived." (Vice-President of the United States)

"I pray Heaven to bestow the best blessings on this house and all that shall hereafter inhabit. May none but honest and wise men ever rule under this roof."

"As much as I converse with sages and heroes, they have very little of my love and admiration. I long for rural and domestic scene, for the warbling of birds and the prattling of my children."

"Abuse of words has been the great instrument of sophistry and chicanery, of party, faction, and division of society."

03. THOMAS JEFFERSON (1801-1809)

"One man with courage is a majority."

"That government is best which governs the least, because its people discipline themselves."

"The price of freedom is eternal vigilance."

"I have sworn upon the altar of God, eternal hostility against every form of tyranny over the mind of man."

"That government is best which governs the least, because its people discipline themselves."

"Nothing gives one person so much advantage over another as to remain always cool and unruffled under all circumstances."

"No duty the Executive had to perform was so trying as to put the right man in the right place.

"I like the dreams of the future better than the history of the past."

"I cannot live without books."

"I wish it were possible to (amend our) constitution with... an additional articles taking from the federal government the power of borrowing."

"I'm a great believer in luck, and I find the harder I work the more I have of it."

"Nothing can stop the man with the right mental attitude from achieving his goal; nothing on earth can help the man with the wrong mental attitude."

"Rebellion to tyrants is obedience."

"Indeed, I tremble for my country when I reflect that God is just; that his justice cannot sleep forever."

"Enlighten the people generally, and tyranny and oppressions of body and mind will vanish like evil spirits at the dawn of day."

"I would rather be exposed to the inconveniences attending too much liberty than those attending too small a degree of it."

"If a nation expects to be ignorant and free…it expect what never was and never will be."

"Our liberty depends on the freedom of the press, and that cannot be limited without being lost."

"The earth is given as a common for men to labor and live in."

"The God who gave us life gave us liberty at the same time."

"The happiest moments of my life have been the few which I have passed at home in the bosom of my family…public employment contributes neither to advantage nor happiness. It is but honorable exile from one's family and affairs."

"The man who fears no truths has nothing to fear from lies."

"The tree of liberty must be refreshed from time to time with the blood of patriots and tyrants. It is it's natural manure."

"We are not to expect to be translated from despotism to liberty in a feather bed."

"We hold these truths to be self-evident, that all men are created equal, that they are endowed by their Creator with certain inalienable rights, that among these are, life, liberty and the pursuit of happiness."

"Were it left to me to decide whether we should have a government without newspapers, or newspapers without a government, I should not hesitate a moment to prefer the latter."

"It is neither wealth nor splendor, but tranquility and occupation, that gives happiness."

"A little rebellion now and then is a good thing, and as necessary in the political world as storms in the physical."

"The God who gave us life, gave us liberty at the same time."

"In matters of style swim with the current, in matters of principle, stand like a rock."

"Information is the currency of democracy."

"A democratic depends upon an informed and educated citizenry."

"The Declaration of Independence…(is the) declaratory charter of our rights, and the rights of man."

"The last hopes of human liberty in this world rests on us."

"Nothing is unchangeable but the inherent and inalienable rights of man."

"Timid men…prefer the calm of despotism to the boisterous sea of liberty."

"Eternal vigilance is the price of victory."

"Peace, commerce, and honest friendship with all nations – entangling alliances with none."

"The man who would choose security over freedom deserves neither."

"The constitution of the United States is the result of the collected wisdom of our country."

"The most valuable of all talents is that of never using two words when one will do."

"When angry, count ten before you speak, if very angry, count a hundred."

"The selfish spirit of commerce, which knows no country, and feels no passion or principle but that of gain."

"I hope our wisdom will grow with our power, and teach us, that the less we use our power the greater it will be."

"No government ought to be without censors; and where the press is free no one ever will."

"I have not observed men's honesty to increase with their riches."

"The boisterous sea of liberty is never without a wave."

04. JAMES MADISON (1809-1817)

"The truth is that all men having power ought to be mistrusted."

"The problem to be solved is, not what form of government is perfect, but which of the forms is least imperfect."

"Since the general civilization of mankind, I believe there are more instances of the abridgement of the freedom of the people by gradual and silent encroachments of those in power than by violent and sudden usurpations."

"A popular Government, without popular information, or the means of acquiring it, is but a Prologue to a Farce or a Tragedy, or, perhaps both. Knowledge will forever govern ignorance. And a people who mean to be their own Governors, must arm themselves with the power which knowledge gives."

"Learned institutions ought to be favorite objects with every free people. They throw that light over the public mind which is the best security against crafty and dangerous encroachments on the public liberty."

"The essence of Government is power; and power, lodged as if it must be in human hands, will ever be liable to abuse."

"No nation could preserve its freedom in the midst of continual warfare."

"What is government itself but the greatest of all reflections on human nature? If men were angels, no government would be necessary. If angels were to govern men, neither external nor internal controls on government would be necessary."

"The growing wealth acquired by them (corporations) never fails to be a source of abuses."

"All power in human hands is liable to be abused."

"Perhaps it is a universal truth that the loss of liberty at home is to be charges to provisions against danger, real or pretended, from abroad."

"No government any more than an individual will long be respected without being truly respectable."

"It is vain to say that enlightened statesmen will always be able to adjust their interests. Enlightened men will not always be at the helm."

"The President is responsible to the public for the conduct of the person he has nominated and appointed."

"The advice nearest to my heart and deepest in my convictions is that the Union of the States be cherished and perpetuated."

"Do not separate text from historical background. If you do, you will have perverted and subverted the Constitution, which can only end in a distorted, bastardization form of illegitimate government."

"Liberty may be endangered by the abuse of Liberty, but also by the abuse of power."

"In framing a government, which is to be administered by man over men, the great difficulty lies in this: you must first enable the government to control the governed, and in the next place, oblige it to control itself."

"Government destitute of energy, will ever produce anarchy."

"History records that the money changers have used every form of abuse, intrigue, deceit, and violent means possible to maintain their control over governments by controlling the money and its issuance."

"It will be of little avail to the people that the laws are made by men of their own choice if the Laws be so voluminous that they cannot be read, or so incoherent that they cannot be understood."

"I cannot undertake to lay my finger on that article of the Constitution which granted a right to Congress of expending, on the objects of benevolence, the money of their constituents."

"The means of defense against foreign danger historically have become the instruments of tyranny at home."

05. JAMES MONROE (1817-1825)

"National honor is a national property of the highest value."

"The American continents ... are henceforth not to be considered as subjects for future colonization by any European powers."

"A little flattery will support a man through great fatigue."

"A free, virtuous, and enlightened people must know full well the great principles and causes upon which their happiness depends."

"The earth was given to mankind to support the greatest number of which it is capable, and no tribe or people have a right to withhold from the wants of others more than is necessary for their own support and comfort."

"Of the liberty of conscience in matters of religious faith, of speech and of the press; of the trial by jury of the vicinage in civil and criminal cases; of the benefit of the writ of habeas corpus; of the right to keep and bear arms…if these rights are well defined, and secured against encroachment, it is impossible that government should ever degenerate into tyranny."

"When we view the great blessing with which our country has been favored, those which we now enjoy, and the means which we posses of handling them down unimpaired to our latest posterity, our attention is irresistibly down to the source from whence they flow. Let us, then, unite in offering our most grateful acknowledgements for those blessing to the Divine Author of All Good."

"In a republic, it is not the people themselves who make the decisions, but the people they themselves choose to stand in their places."

"In this great nation there is but one order, that of the people, whose power, by a peculiarly happy improvement of the representation principle, is transferred from them, without impairing in the slightest degree their sovereignty, to bodies of their own creation, and to persons elected by themselves, in the full extent necessary for the purposes of free, enlightened, and efficient government."

06. JOHN QUINCY ADAMS (1825-1829)

"This mode of electioneering suited neither my taste nor my principles. I thought it equally unsuitable to my personal character and to the station in which I am placed."

"May our country be always successful, but whether successful or otherwise, always right."

"America, with the same voice which spoke herself into existence as a nation, proclaimed to mankind the inextinguishable rights of human nature, and the only lawful foundations of government."

"Always vote for principle, though you may vote alone, and you may cherish the sweetest reflection that your vote is never lost."

"Patience and Perseverance have a magical effect before which difficulties disappear and obstacles vanish."

"The declaration that our People are hostile to a government made by themselves, for themselves, and conducted by themselves, is an insult."

"The influence of each human being on others in this life is a kind of immortality."

"Old minds are like old horses, you must exercise them if you wish to keep them in working order."

"No stones, nor wood, not the art of artisans make a state; but where men are who know how to take care of themselves, these are cities and walls."

"Where annual elections end, there slavery begins."

"Individual liberty is individual power, and as the power of a community is a mass compounded of individual powers, the nation which enjoys the most freedom must necessarily be in proportion to its numbers the most powerful nation."

"The laws of man may bind him in chains or may put him to death, but they never make him wide, virtuous, or happy."

"Civil liberty can be established on no foundation of human reason which will not at the same time demonstrate the right of religious freedom."

"If your actions inspire others to dream more, learn more, do more and become more, you are a leader."

"Posterity – you will never know how much it has cost my generation to preserve your freedom. I hope you will make good use of it."

"Yesterday the greatest question was decided which was ever debated in America; and a greater perhaps never was; nor will be, decided among men. A resolution was passed without one dissenting colony, that those United Colonies are, an of right ought to be, free and independent States.

"So great is my veneration for the Bible, that the earlier my children begin to read it the more confident will be my hopes that they will prove useful citizens to their country and respectable members of society."

"All men profess honesty as long as they can. To believe all men hones would be folly. To believe none so is something worse."

"Courage and perseverance have a magical talisman, before which difficulties disappear and obstacles vanish into air."

"Duty is ours; results are God's."

"Idle is sweet, and its consequences are cruel."

"This is the last of earth! I am content.

07. ANDREW JACKSON (1829-1837)

"The Individual who refuses to defend his rights when called by his government, deserves to be a slave, and must be punished as an enemy of his country and friend to her foe."

"I know what I am fit for. I can command a body of men in a rough way; but I am not fit to be president."

"Internal improvement and the diffusion of knowledge, so far as they can be promoted by the constitutional acts of the Federal Government, are of high importance."

"Any man worth his salt will stick up for what he believes right, but it takes a slightly better man to acknowledge instantly and without reservation that he is in error."

"Never take counsel of your fear."

"Our Federal Union: it must be preserved."

"One man with courage makes a majority."

"The Bible is the rock on which our Republic rests."

"There are no necessary evils in government. Its evils exist only in its abuses."

"To the victors belong the spoils."

"There is no pleasure in having nothing to do; the fun is having lots to do and not doing it."

"But you must remember, my fellow-citizens, the eternal vigilance by the people is the price of liberty, and that you must pay the price if you wish to secure the blessing. It behooves you, therefore, to be watchful in your States as well as in the Federal Government."

"Never sue for assault or slander, settle them cases yourself."

"I am one of those who do not believe that a national debt is a national blessing, but rather a curse to a republic, inasmuch as it is calculated to raise around the administration a moneyed aristocracy dangerous to the liberties of the country."

"Take time to deliberate; but when the time for action arrives, stop thinking and go in."

"Any man worth his salt will stick up for what he believes right, but it takes a slightly better man to acknowledge instantly and without reservation that he is in error."

"It is to be regretted that the rich and powerful too often bend the acts of government to their selfish purposes."

"It is a damn poor mind indeed which can't think of at least two ways to spell any word."

"The wisdom of man never yet contrived a system of taxation that would operate with perfect equality."

"Heaven will be no heaven to me if I do not meet my wife there."

08. MARTIN VAN BUREN (1837-1841)

"Unlike all who have preceded me, the Revolution that gave us existence as one people was achieved at the period of my birth; and whilst I contemplate with grateful reverence that memorable event, I feel that I belong to a later age and that I may not expect my countrymen to weigh my actions with the same kind and partial hand."

"For myself, therefore, I desire to declare that the principle that will govern me in the high duty to which my country calls me is a strict adherence to the letter and spirit of the Constitution as it was designed by those who framed it."

"I cannot expect to perform the task with equal ability and success." (Martin Van Buren taking over from Andrew Jackson in 1837)

"Those who look to the action of this government for specific aid to the citizen to relieve embarrassments arising from losses by revulsions in commerce and credit, lose sight of the ends for which it was created, and the powers with which it is clothed. It was established to give security to us all….It was not intended to confer special favors on individuals. The less government interferes with private pursuits, the better for the general prosperity."

"It is easier to do a job right than to explain why you didn't."

"I tread in the footsteps of illustrious men, whose superiors it is our happiness to believe are not found on the executive calendar of any country."

"As to the Presidency, the two happiest days of my life were those of my entrance upon the office and my surrender of it."

"There is a power in public opinion in this country – and I thank God for it: for it is the most honest and best of all powers which will not tolerate an incompetent or unworthy man to hold in his weak or wicked hands the lives and fortunes of his fellow-citizens."

"All forms of religion have united for the first time to diffuse charity and piety, because for the first time in the history of nations all have been totally untrammeled and absolutely free."

09. WILLIAM HENRY HARRISON (1841)

"The prudent capitalist will never adventure his capital … if there exists a state of uncertainty as to whether the Government will repeal tomorrow what it has enacted today."

"A decent and manly examination of the acts of the Government should be not only tolerated, but encouraged."

"But I contend that the strongest of all governments is that which is most free."

"We Americans have no commission from God to police the world."

"We admit of no government by divine right, the only legitimate right to govern is an express grant of power from the governed."

"Sir, I wish to understand the true principles of the Government. I wish them carried out. I ask nothing more."

"The plea of necessity, that eternal argument of all conspirators."

"I believe and I say it is true Democratic feeling, that all the measures of the government are directed to the purpose of making the right richer and the poor poorer."

"The people are the best guardians of their own rights and it is the duty of their executive to abstain from interfering in or thwarting the sacred exercise of the lawmaking functions of their government."

"There is nothing more corrupting, nothing more destructive of the noblest and finest feelings of our nature, than the exercise of unlimited power."

"I proceed to state in as summary a manner as I can my opinion of the sources of the evils which have been so extensively complained of…Some of the former are unquestionably to be found in the defects of the Constitution; others, in my judgment, are attributable to a misconstruction of some of its provisions. Of the former is the eligibility of the same individual to a second term of the Presidency."

"Times change, and we change with them."

"Our citizens must be content with the existence of the powers with which the Constitution clothes them."

"We admit of no government by divine right…The only legitimate right to govern is an express grant of power from the governed."

10. JOHN TYLER (1841-1845)

"I can never consent to being dictated to."

"Popularity, I have always thought, may aptly be compared to a coquette-the more you woo her, the more apt is she to elude your embrace."

"Wealth can only be accumulated by the earnings of industry and the savings of frugality."

"Let it be henceforth proclaimed to the world that man's conscience was created free; that he is no longer accountable to his fellow man for his religious opinions, being responsible therefore only to his God."

"Here lies the body of my good horse, "The General." For twenty years he bore me around the circuit of my practice, and in all that time he never made a blunder. Would that his master could say the same!

"In 1840, I was called from my farm to undertake the administration of public affairs and I foresaw that I was called to a bed of thorns. I now leave that bed which has afforded me little rest, and eagerly seek repose in the quiet enjoyments of rural life." (Explaining why he would not run for reelection.)

"It is easier to do a job right than to explain why you didn't."

"If the tide of defamation and abuse shall turn, and my administration come to be praised, future Vice-Presidents who may succeed to the Presidency may feel some slight encouragement to pursue an independent course."

"I am going.... .Perhaps it is best." (His last words at his death)

"The institutions under which we live, my countrymen, secure each person in the perfect enjoyment of all his rights."

"Patronage is the sword and cannon by which war may be made on the ;iberty of the human race."

"So far as it depends on the course of this government, our relations of good will and friendship will be sedulously cultivated with all nations."

"Popularity, I have always thought, may aptly be compared to a coquette – the more you woo herm the more apt is she to elude your embrace."

11. JAMES KNOX POLK (1845-1849)

"With me it is exceptionally true that the Presidency is no bed of roses."

"Public opinion: May it always perform one of its appropriate offices, by teaching the public functionaries of the State and of the Federal Government, that neither shall assume the exercise of powers entrusted by the Constitution to the other."

"I am heartily rejoiced that my term is so near its close. I will soon cease to be a servant and will become a sovereign."

"Peace, plenty, and contentment reign throughout our borders, and our beloved country presents a sublime moral spectacle to the world..."

"No president who performs his duties faithfully and conscientiously can have any leisure."

"Mr. Buchanan is a man of talents and is fully competent to discharge the high duties of Secretary of State, but it is one of his weaknesses (and perhaps all great men have such) that he takes on and magnifies small matters into great and undeserved importance." (Future President)

"The passion for office among members of Congress is very great, if not absolutely disreputable, and greatly embarrasses the operations of the Government. They create offices by their own votes and then seek to fill them themselves."

"There is more selfishness and less principle among members of Congress…than I had any conception of, before I became President of the U.S."

"One great object of the Constitution was to restrain majorities from oppressing minorities or encroaching upon their just rights. Minorities have a right to appeal to the Constitution as a shield against such oppression."

"Foreign powers do not seem to appreciate the true character of our government."

"Under the blessings of Divine Providence… It becomes us in humility to make our devout acknowledgments to the Supreme Rule of the Universe for the inestimable civil and religious blessings with which we are favored."

"I cannot, whilst President of the United States, descend to enter into a newspaper controversy."

"It [the US Government] is a common protector of each and all the States; of every man who lives upon our soil, whether of native or foreign birth; of every religious sect, in their worship of the Almighty according to the dictates of their own conscience; of every shade of opinion, and the most free inquiry; of every art, trade, and occupation consistent with the laws of the States."

"Well may the boldest fear and the wisest tremble when incurring responsibilities on which may defend our country's peace and prosperity, and in some degree the hopes and happiness of the whole human family."

"I prefer to supervise the whole operations of Government myself rather than entrust the public business to subordinate and this makes my duties very great."

12. ZACHERY TAYLOR (1849-1850)

"For more than half a century, during which kingdoms and empires have fallen, this Union has stood unshaken. The patriots who formed it have long since descended to the grave; yet still it remains, the proudest monument to their memory …"

"It would be judicious to act with magnanimity towards a prostrate foe."

"The idea that I should become President seems to me too visionary to require a serious answer. It has never entered my head, nor is it likely to enter the head of any other person."

"In the discharge of duties my guide will be the Constitution, which I this day swear to preserve, protect, and defend."

"…I can and shall yield to no call that does not come from the spontaneous action and free will of the nation at large and void of the slightest agency of my own … In no cases can I permit myself to be a candidate of any part, or yield my self to any party schemes."

"I have no private purpose to accomplish, no party objectives to build up, no enemies to punish-nothing to serve but my country."

"In the discharge of duties my guide will be the Constitution, which I this day swear to preserve, protect, and defend."

"It would be judicious to act with magnanimity towards a prostrate foe."

"I have always done my duty. I am ready to die. My only regret is for the friends I leave behind me."

"For more than half a century, during which Kingdoms and empires have fallen, this Union has stood unshaken. The patriots who formed it have long since descended to the grave; yet still it remains, the proudest monument to their memory."

"Tell him to go to hell." (His reply to Mexican General Santa Anna's demand for surrender)

"Upon its preservation [the United States] must depend on our own happiness and that of countless generations to come. Whatever dangers may threaten it, I shall stand by it and maintain it in its integrity to the full extent of the obligations imposed and the power conferred upon me by the Constitution." (1849)

"In conclusion, I congratulate you, my fellow-citizens, upon the high state of prosperity to which the goodness of Divine Providence has conducted our common country. Let us invoke a continuance of the same protecting care which has led us from small beginnings to the eminence we this day occupy."

"I am a Whig, but not an ultra-Whig."

"The power given by the Constitution to the Executive to interpose his veto is a high conservative power; but in my opinion it should never be exercised except in cases of clear violation of the Constitution, or manifest haste and want of due consideration by Congress."

"I wish my plantation and servants kept together for ten years, and after paying the several legacies referred to, the net proceeds of my crops to be equally divided between my two daughters ... I wish the servants only moderately worked and kindly treated, and the old ones taken care of and made comfortable, which I hope my children have attended to... . I give my daughter Mary Elizabeth , . . the servant woman Mary, a slave for Life, ... and her four children, forever, to dispose of as she may think proper."

13. MILLARD FILLMORE (1850-1853)

"It is not strange … to mistake change for progress."

"An honorable defeat is better than a dishonorable victory."

"The man who can look upon a crises without being willing to offer himself upon the altar of his country is not for public trust."

'Nothing brings out the lower traits of human nature like office-seeking. Men of good character and impulses are betrayed by it into all sorts of meanness."

"It is a national disgrace that our Presidents, after having occupied the highest position in the country, should be cast adrift, and perhaps, be compelled to keep a corner grocery for subsistence."

"Let us remember that revolutions do not always establish freedom. Our own free institutions were not the offspring of our Revolution. They existed before."

"The man who can look upon a crisis without being willing to offer himself upon the altar of his country is not fit for public trust."

14. FRANKLIN PIERCE (1853-1857)

"We have nothing in our history or position to invite aggression; we have everything to beckon us to the cultivation of relations of peace and amity with all nations."

"The storm of frenzy and faction must inevitably dash itself in vain against the unshaken rock of the Constitution."

"The revenue of the country, levied almost insensibly to the taxpayer, goes on from year to year, increasing beyond either the interests or the prospective wants of the Government."

"Frequently the more trifling the subject the more animated and protracted the discussion."

"The stars upon your banner have become nearly threefold their original number; your densely populated possessions skirt the shores of the two great oceans."

"You have summoned me in my weakness. You must sustain me by your strength."

"The dangers of a concentration of all power in the general government of a confederacy so vast as ours are too obvious to be disregarded." (Inaugural Address, March 4, 1853)

"I wish I could indulge higher hope for the future of our country, but the aspect of any vision is fearfully dark and I cannot make it otherwise." (During the secession crises of 1860)

"Remember that time is money."

"Frequently the more trifling the subject, the more animated and protracted the discussion."

"With the Union my best and dearest earthly hopes are entwined."

15. JAMES BUCHANAN (1857-1861)

"Liberty must be allowed to work out its natural result; and these will, are long, astonish the world."

"Our union rests upon public opinion, and can never be cememnted by the blood of its citizens shed in civil war."

"The distribution of patronage of the Government is by far the most disagreeable duty of the President."

"What is right and what is practicable are two different things."

"To avoid entangling alliances has been a maxim of our policy ever since the days of Washington, and its wisdoms no one will attempt to dispute."

"The ballot box is the surest arbiter of disputes among freemen."

"There is nothing stable but Heaven and the Constitution."

"Abstract propositions should never be discussed by a legislative body."

"We must have Cuba; we can't do without Cuba ..."

"I like the noise of democracy."

"Prevent the American people from crossing the Rocky Mountain? You might as well command Niagara not to flow. We must fulfill our destiny."

"The test of leadership is not to put greatness into humanity, but to elicit it, for the greatness is already there."

"If you are as happy in entering the White House as I shall feel on returning to Wheatland, you are a happy man, indeed."

"Whatever the result may be, I shall carry to my grave the consciousness that I at least meant well for my country."

16. ABRAHAM LINCOLN (1861-1865)

"Let the people know the truth and the country is safe."

"I have never had a feeling politically that did not spring from the sentiments embodied in the Declaration of Independence."

"Always bear in mind that your own resolution to success is more important than any other one thing."

"In giving freedom to the slave, we assure freedom to the free – honorable alike in what we give, and what we preserve. We shall nobly save, or meanly lose, the last best hope of earth. Other means may succeed; this could not fail. The way is plain, peaceful, generous, just - a

"Nearly all men can stand adversity, but if you want to test a man's character, give him power."

"You can fool all of the people some of the time, and some of the people all of the time, but you can not fool all of the people all of the time."

"Freedom is not the right to do what we want, but what we ought. Let us have faith that right makes might and in that faith let us, to the end, dare to do our duty as we understand it."

"If slavery is not wrong, nothing is wrong."

"We here highly resolve that this nation, under God, shall have a new birth of freedom, and that government of the people, by the people, for the people, shall not perish from the earth."

"Common looking people are the best in the world: that is the reason the Lord makes so many of them."

"On the whole, my impression is that mercy bears richer fruits than any other attribute."

"I believe the Bible is the best gift God has ever given to men. All the good the Savior gave to the world was communicated through this book."

"Upon the subject of education, not presuming to dictate any plan or system respecting it, I can only say that I view it as the most important subject which we as a people can be engaged in."

"Things may come to those who wait, but only the things left by those who hustle."

"I think that God means that we shall do more than we have yet done in furtherance of his plans and he will open the way for our doing it."

"If I had eight hours to chop down a tree, I'd spend six sharpening my axe."

"If you look for the bad in people expecting to find it, you surely will."

"I shall try to correct errors where shown to be errors, and I shall adopt new views as fast as they shall appear to be true views."

"Important principles may and must be inflexible."

"I claim not to have controlled events, but confess plainly that events have controlled me."

"Do I not destroy my enemies when I make them my friends."

"I am naturally anti-slavery. If slavery is not wrong, nothing is wrong. I can not remember when I did not so think, and feel. Any yet I have never understood that the Presidency conferred upon me an unrestricted right to act officially upon this judgment and feeling."

"My best friend is a person who will give me a book I have not read."

"Our reliance is in the love of liberty...Our defense is in the preservation of the spirit which prizes liberty as the heritage of all men, in all lands, everywhere."

"The better part of one's life consists of friendships."

"Let us have faith that right makes might, and in that faith, let us, to the end, dare to do our duty as we understand it."

"My concern is not whether God is on our side, my great concern is to be on God's side."

"Tact is the ability to describe others as they see themselves."

"We have highly resolve that these dead shall not have died in vain; that this nation shall have a new birth of freedom."

"...that government of the people, by the people, for the people, shall not perish from this earth."

"My great concern is not whether you have failed, but whether you are content with your failure."

"The best thing about the future is that it comes only one day at a time."

"As I would not be a slave, so I would not be a master. This expresses my idea of democracy. Whatever differs from this, to the extent of the difference, is no democracy."

"I have never studied the art of paying compliments to women; but I must say that if all that has been said by orators and poets since the creation of the world in praise of women were applied to the women of America, it would not do them justice for their conduct during this war. I will close by saying, God bless the women of America." (Remarks at Closing of Sanitary Fair, Washington, D.C., March 18, 1864)

"Let us at all times remember that all American citizens are brothers of the common country, and should dwell together in bonds of fraternal feeling."

"Most folks are about as happy as they make up their minds to be."

"Must a government of necessity be too strong for the liberties of its people or too weak to maintain its own existence?"

"No man is good enough to govern another man without that other's consent."

"The probability that we may fail in the struggle ought not to deter us from the support of a cause we believe to be just."

"Those who deny freedom to others deserve it not for themselves, and, under a just God, cannot long retain it."

"When you have got an elephant by the hind leg, and he is trying to run away, it's best to let him run."

"In giving freedom to the slave we assure freedom to the free honorable alike in what we give and why."

"You cannot build character and courage by taking away a man's initiative and independence."

"America will never be destroyed from the outside. If we falter and lose our freedoms, it will be because we destroyed ourselves."

"It is a sin to be silent when it is your duty to protest."

"And in the end, it's not the years in your life that count. It's the life in your years."

"Die when I may, I want it said of me that I plucked a weed and planted a flower whenever I thought a flower would grow."

17. ANDREW JOHNSON (1865-1869)

"Washington, DC is 12 square miles bordered by reality."

"I have reached the summit of my ambition."

"If the rabble were lopped off at one end and the aristocrat at the other, all would be well with the country."

"Honest conviction is my courage; the Constitution is my guide."

"The goal to strive for is a poor government but a rich people."

"There are no good laws but such as repeal other laws."

"Let peace and prosperity be restored to the land. May God bless this people: may God save the Constitution."

"We have no legal authority more than private citizens, and within it we have only so much as that instrument gives us. This broad principle limits all our functions and applies to all subjects."

"Honest conviction is my courage; the Constitution is my guide."

"I hold it the duty of the executive to insist upon frugality in the expenditure, and a sparing economy is itself a great national source."

"The goal to strive for is a poor government but a rich people."

"Legislation can neither be wise nor just which seeks the welfare of a single interest at the expense and to the injury of many and varied interests."

"I have been almost overwhelmed by the announcement of the sad event [Lincoln's Assassination] which has so recently occurred. I feel incompetent to perform duties so important and responsible as those which have been so unexpectedly thrown upon me." (Assassination of Abraham Lincoln)

"I am sworn to uphold the Constitution as Andy Johnson understands it and interprets it."

"Tyranny and despotism can be exercised by many, more rigorously, more vigorously, and more severely, than by one."

"The times we live in are not without instruction. The American people must be taught – if they do not already feel – that treason is a crime and must be punished; that the Government will not always bear with its enemies; that it is strong not only to protect but to punish."

"I have performed my duty to my God, my country, and my family. I have nothing to fear in approaching death. To me it is the mere shadow of God's protecting wing ... . Here I will rest in quiet and peace beyond the reach of calumny's poisoned shaft, the influence of envy and jealous enemies, where treason and traitors or State backsliders and hypocrites in church can have no peace." (Written just before his death in July 1985)

18. ULYSSES SIMPSON GRANT (1869-1877)

"It was my fortune, or misfortune, to be called to the office of Chief Executive without any previous political training."

"In politics I am growing indifferent – I would like it, if I could now return to my planting and books at home."

"It is men who wait to be elected, and not those who seek, from whom we may expect the most efficient service."

"I know only two tunes: one of them is "Yankee Doodle," and the other isn't."

"I have never advocated war except as a means of peace."

"My failures have been errors of judgment, not of intent."

"Every human being, of whatever origin, of whatever station, deserves respect. We must each respect others even as we respect ourselves."

"The Southern Rebellion was largely the outgrowth of the Mexican War. Nations, like individuals are punished for their transgressions. We got our punishment in the most sanguinary and expensive war of modern times."

"I have acted in every instance from a conscientious desire to do what was right, constitutional, within the law, and for the very best interests of the whole people. Failures have been errors of judgment, not of intent."

"If men make war in slavish obedience to rules, they will fail."

"The right of revolution is an inherent one. When people are oppressed by their government, it is a natural right they enjoy to relieve themselves of oppression, if they are strong enough, whether by withdrawal from it, or by overthrowing it and substituting a government more acceptable."

"I know no method to secure the repeal of bad or obnoxious laws so effective as their stringent execution."

"The friend in my adversity I shall always cherish most. I can better trust those who helped to relieve the gloom of my dark hours than those who are so ready to enjoy with me the sunshine of my prosperity."

"Leave the matter of religion to the family altar; the church, and the private school, supported entirely by private contributions. Keep the church and state forever separate."

"Everyone has his substituting. One of mine has always been when I started to go anywhere, or to do anything, never to turn back or to stop until the thing intended was accomplished."

"Labor disgraces no man; unfortunately, you occasionally find men who disgrace labor."

"The right of revolution is an inherent one. When people are oppressed by their government, it is a natural right they enjoy to relieve themselves of the oppression, if they are strong enough, whether by withdrawal from it, or by overthrowing it and substituting a government more acceptable."

"Let no guilty man escape, if it can be avoided... . no personal consideration should stand in the way of performing a public duty."

"There never was a time when, in my opinion, some way could not be found to prevent the drawing of a sword."

19. RUTHERFORD B. HAYES (1877-1881)

"The President of the United States of necessity owes his election to office to the suffrage and zealous labors of a political party,... but he should strive to be always mindful of the fact that he serves his party best who serves the country best."

"I am not liked as a President by the politicians in office, in the press, or in Congress. But I am content to abide the judgment – the sober second thought – of the people."

"It will be the duty of the Executive, with sufficient appropriations for the purpose, to prosecute unsparingly all who have been engaged in depriving citizens of the rights guaranteed to them by the Constitution."

"Fighting battles is like courting girls: those who make the most pretensions and are boldest usually win."

"In avoiding the appearance of evil, I am not sure but I have sometimes unnecessarily deprived myself and others of innocent enjoyments."

"There can be no complete and permanent reform of the civil service until public opinion emancipates congressmen from all control and influence over government patronage ... No proper legislation is to be expected as long as members of Congress are engaged in procuring offices for their constituents."

"Nothing brings out the lower traits of human nature like office seeking."

"He serves his party best who serves the country best."

"I would honor the man who would give to his country a good newspaper."

"May policy is trust-peace, and to put aside the bayonet."

"Abolish plutocracy if you would abolish poverty."

"Virtue is defined to be mediocrity, of which either extreme is vice."

"It is now true that this is God's Country, if equal rights-a fair start and an equal chance in the race of life are everywhere secured to all."

"The melancholy thing in our public life is the insane desire to get higher."

"Nothing brings out the lower traits of human nature like office-seeking. Men of good character and impulses are betrayed by it into all sorts of meanness."

"An amazing invention (telephone) – but who would ever want to use one?"

"Coming in, I was denounced as a fraud by all the extreme men of the opposing party, and as an ingrate and a traitor by the same class of men in my own party. Going out, I have the good will, blessings, and approval of the best people of all parties...."

"I know that I am going where Lucy is." (His last words about his wife at his death in January of 1893)

20. JAMES A. GARFIELD (1881)

"The President is the last person in the world to know what the people really want and think."

"The truth will set you free, but first it will make you miserable."

"If the power to do hard work is not a skill, it's the best possible substitute for it."

"I mean to make myself a man, and if I succeed in that, I shall succeed in everything else."

"History is philosophy teaching by example, and also warning; its two eyes are geography and chronology."

"The civil service can never be placed on a satisfactory basis until it is regulated by law."

"Ideas control the world."

"Be fit for more than the thing you are now doing. Let everyone know that you have a reserve in yourself; that you have more power than you are now using. If you are not too large for the place you occupy, you are too small for it."

"If wrinkles must be written upon our brows, let them not be written upon the heart. The spirit should not grow old."

"Whoever controls the volume of money in any country is absolute master of all industry and commerce."

"All free governments are managed by the combined wisdom and folly of the people."

"Next, in importance to freedom and justice is popular education, without which neither freedom nor justice can be permanently maintained."

"Nothing brings out the lower traits of human nature like office-seeking. Men of good character and impulses are betrayed by it into all sorts of meanness."

"I have had many troubles in my life, but the worst of them never came."

"We can not overestimate the fervent love of liberty, the intelligent courage, and the sum of common sense with which our fathers made the great experiment of self-government."

"Whoever controls the volume of money in any country is absolute master of all industry and commerce."

"A pound of pluck is worth a ton of luck."

"All free governments are managed by the combined wisdom and folly of the people."

21. CHESTER A. ARTHUR (1881-1885)

"Since I came here I have learned that Chester A. Arthur is one man and the President of the United States is another."

"The Office of Vice-President is a greater honor than I ever dreamed of attaining."

"Honors to me now are not what they once were."

"I don't think we had better go into the minute secrets of the campaign, so far as I know them, because I see the reporters are present, who are talking it all down. If it were not for the reporters, I would tell you the truth."

"Good ballplayers make good citizens."

"The extravagant expenditure of public money is an evil not to be measure by the value of that money to the people who are taxed for it."

"If it were not for the reporters, I would tell you the truth."

"Men may die, but the fabrics of our free institutions remain unshaken."

"A man my age has nothing left to do but move to the country and grow big pumpkins."

22. GROVER CLEVELAND (1885-1889)
(also 24th president)

"I am honest and sincere in my desire to do well, but the question is whether I know enough to accomplish what I desire."

"Honor lies in honest toil."

"There is no calamity which a great nation can invite which equals that which follows a supine submission to wrong and injustice and the consequent loss of national self-respect and honor, beneath which are shielded and defended a people's safety and greatness."

"A government for the people must depend for its success on the intelligence, the morality, the injustice, and the interest of the people themselves."

"Officeholders are the agents of the people, not their masters."

"A man is known by the company he keeps, and also by the company from which he is kept out."

"Above all, tell the truth."

"It is the responsibility off the citizens to support their government. It is not the responsibility of the government to support its citizens.

"A truly American sentiment recognizes the dignity of labor and the fact that honor lies in honest toil."

"Though the people support the government, the government should not support the people."

23. BENJAMIN HARRISON (1889 – 1893)

"Great lives never go out; they go on."

"The bud of victory is always in the truth."

"I have often though that the life of the President is like that of the policeman in the opera, not a happy one."

"I knew that my staying up would not change the election result if I were defeated, while if elected I had a hard day ahead of me. So, I thought a night's rest was best in any event."

"No other people have a government more worthy of their respect and love or a land so magnificent in extent, so pleasant to look upon, and so full of generous suggestion to enterprise and labor."

"Columbus stood in his age as the pioneer of progress and achievement. The system of universal education is in our age the most prominent and salutary feature of the spirit of enlightenment, and it is peculiarly appropriate that the schools be made by the people the center of the day's demonstration. Let the national flag float over every school-house in the country, and the exercises be such as shall impress upon our youth the patriotic duties of American citizenship."

"Lincoln had faith in time, and time has justified his faith."

"I have only a vague memory of my grandfather as I was only a child when he died, but I will show all my family's famous name is safe in my keeping."

"Will it not be wise to allow the friendship between nations to rest upon deep and permanent things? Irritations of the cuticle must not be confounded with heart failure."

"The Americans have no commission from God to police the world."

"The disfranchisement of a single legal elector by fraud or intimidation is a crime too grave to be regarded lightly."

"Unlike many other people less happy, we give our devotion to a government, to its Constitution, to its flag, and not to men."

"The only legitimate right to govern is an express grant of power from the governed."

"Have you not learned that not stocks or bonds or stately houses, or products of the mill or field are our country? It is a spiritual thought that is in our minds."

"The indiscriminate denunciation of the rich is mischievous.... No poor man was ever made richer or happier by it. It is quite as illogical to despise a man because he is rich as because he is poor. Not what a man has, but what he is, settles his class. We can not right matter by taking from one what he has honestly acquired to bestow upon another, what he has not earned."

"After the heavy blow of the death of my wife, I do not think that I could have stood re-election."

"I do the same thing every day. I eat three meals, sleep six hours and read dusty old book the rest of the time. My life is about as devoid of anything funny as the great desert is of grass."

24. GROVER CLEVELAND (1843-1897) (also 22nd president)

"What is the use of being elected or re-elected unless you stand for something?"

"Party honesty is party expediency."

"The truly American sentiment recognizes the dignity of labor and the fact that honor lies in natural toil."

"Sensible and responsible women do not want to vote."

"The laws should be rigidly enforced which prohibit the immigration of a servile class to compete with American labor, with no intention of acquiring citizenship, and bringing with them and retaining habits and customs repugnant to our civilization."

"Your every voter, as surely as your chief magistrate, exercises a public trust."

"No man has ever been hanged for breaking the spirit of the law."

"I have considered the pension list of the republic a roll of honor."

"A man is known by the company he keeps, and also by the company from which he is kept out."

25. WILLIAM MCKINLEY (1897-1901)

"I have never been in doubt since I was old enough to think intelligently that I would someday be made President."

"The mission of the United States is one of benevolent assimilation."

"Our differences are politics. Our agreements are principles."

"Expositions are the timekeepers of progress."

"The free man cannot be long an ignorant man."

"Let us ever remember that our interest is in concord, not in conflict, and that our real eminence rests in the victories of peace, not those of war."

"Our earnest prayer is that God will graciously vouchsafe prosperity, happiness, and peace to all our neighbors, and like blessings to all the peoples and powers of the earth."

"I am a tariff man, standing on a tariff platform."

"The best way for the Government to maintain its credit is to pay as it goes. Not by resorting to loans, but by keeping out of debt through an adequate income secured by a system of taxation, eternal or internal, or both."

"That's all a man can hope for during his lifetime-to set an example-and when he is dead, to be an inspiration for history."

"Unlike any other nation, here the people rule, and their will is the supreme law. It is sometimes sneeringly said by those who do not like free government, that here we count heads. True, heads are counted, but brains also…"

"In the time of darkest defeat victory may be nearest."

"Business life, whether among ourselves or with other people, is even a sharp struggle for success. It will be none the less so in the future. Without competition we would be clinging to the clumsy antiquated processes of farming and manufacture and the methods of business of long ago, and the twentieth would be no further advanced than the eighteenth century."

"War should never be entered upon until every agency of peace has failed."

"Cuba ought to be free and independent, and the government should be turned over to the Cuban people."

"We need Hawaii just as much and a good deal more than we did California. It is Manifest Destiny."

"War should never be entered upon until every agency of peace has failed."

"Without competition we would be clinging to the clumsy antiquated processes of farming and manufacture and the methods of business of long ago, and the twentieth would be no further advanced than the eighteenth century."

"Illiteracy must be banished from the land if we shall attain that high destiny as the foremost of the enlightened nations of the world which, under Providence, we ought to achieve."

"That's all a man can hope for during his lifetime – to set an example – and when he is dead, to be an inspiration for history."

"Good-bye – good bye, all. It is God's way. His will, not ours, be done. Nearer my God to Thee, nearer to Thee."

26. THEODORE ROOSEVELT (1901-1909)

"To announce that there must be no criticism of the president, or that we are to stand by the president, right or wrong, is not only unpatriotic and servile, but is morally treasonable to the American public."

"Honesty is… an absolute prerequisite to efficient service to the public."

"Speak softly and carry a big stick and you will go far."

"Rhetoric is a poor substitute for action."

"Keep your eyes on the stars and your feet on the ground."

"When you play, play hard. When you work, don't play at all."

"Your attitude about who you are and what you have is a very little thing that makes a very big difference."

"Unless a man is honest we have no right to keep him in public life, it matters not how brilliant his capacity."

"I wish that all Americans would realize that American politics is world politics."

"We can afford to differ on the currency, the tariff and foreign policy, but we cannot afford to differ on the question of honesty if we expect our republic permanently to endure."

"The only man who makes no mistake is a man who does nothing."

"I think there is only one quality worse than hardness of heart, and that is softness of head."

"Do what you can, with what you have, where you are."

"Far better it is to dare things, to win glorious triumphs, even though checkered by failure, than to take rank with those poor spirits who neither enjoy nor suffer much, because they live in the grey twilight that knows not victory nor defeat."

"It is hard to fail, but it is worse to have tried to succeed in this life we get nothing save by effort."

"No man is worth his salt is not ready at all times to risk his well-being, to risk his body, to risk his life, in a great cause."

"The first requisite of a good citizen in this republic of ours is that he should be able and willing to pull his weight."

"Whenever you are asked if you can do a job, tell 'em. "Certainly I can!" – and get busy and find out how to do it."

"The government is us, we are the government, you and I."

"The men and women who have the right ideals…are those who have the courage to strive for the happiness which comes only with labor and effort and self-sacrifice, and those whose joy in life springs in part from power of work and sense of duty."

"The nation behaves well if it treats the natural resources as assets which it must turn over to the next generation increased, and not impaired, in value."

"To educate a man in mind and not in morals is to educate a menace to society."

"Far and away the best prize that life offers is the chance to work hard at work worth doing."

"Get action. Seize the moment. Man was never intended to become an oyster."

"Freedom from effort in the present merely means that there has been effort stored up in the past."

"Order without liberty and liberty without order are equally destructive."

"No man is above the law, and no man is below it."

"Let us speak courteously, deal, fairly, and keep ourselves armed and ready."

"Of course the all-important thing to keep in mind is that if we have not both strength and virtue we shall fail."

"Our average fellow-citizen is a sane and healthy man, who believes in decency and has a wholesome mind."

"The country needs and, unless I mistake its temper, the country demands bold, persistent experimentation. It is common sense to take a method and try it, if it fails, admit it frankly and try another. But above all, try something.

"There has never yet been a man in our history who led a life of ease whose name is worth remembering."

"The first requisite of a good citizen in this republic of ours is that he shall be able and willing to pull his weight."

"The most successful politician says what everybody is thinking most often and in the loudest voice."

"To discriminate against a thoroughly upright citizen because he belongs to some particular church, or because, like Abraham Lincoln, he has not avowed his allegiance to any church, is an outrage against that liberty of conscience which is one of the foundations of American life."

27. WILLIAM HOWARD TAFT (1909-1913)

"Don't sit up nights thinking about making me President for that will never come and I have no ambition in that direction. Any party which would nominate me would make me a great mistake."

"The intoxication of power rapidly sobers off in the knowledge of its restrictions and under the prompt reminder of an ever-present and not always considerate press, as well as the kindly suggestions that not infrequently come from Congress."

"Politics, when I am in it, makes me sick."

"The trouble with me is that I like to talk too much."

"Presidents come and go, but the Supreme Court goes on, forever."

"Next to the right of liberty, the right of property is the most important individual right guaranteed by the Constitution and the one which, united with that of personal liberty, has contributed more to the growth of civilization than any other institution established by the human race."

"The President cannot make clouds to rain and cannot make the corn to grow, he cannot make business good; although when these things occur, political parties do claim some credit for the good things that have happened in this way."

"I have come to the conclusion that the major part of the work of a President is to go to expositions and fairs and bring tourists to town."

"As the Republican platform says, the welfare of the farmer is vital to that of the whole country."

"Don't worry over what the newspapers say. I don't. Why should anyone else? I told the truth to the newspaper correspondents – but when you tell the truth to them they are at sea."

"We live in a stage of politics, where legislators seem to regard the passage of laws as much more important than the results of their enforcement."

"The intoxication of power rapidly sobers off in the knowledge of its restrictions and under the prompt reminder of an ever-present and not always considerate press, as well as the kindly suggestions that not infrequently come from Congress."

"George Washington intended this to be a Federal city (Washington, DC), and it is a Federal city, and it tingles down to the feet of every man, whether he comes from Washington State, or Los Angeles, or Texas, when he comes and walks these city streets and begins to feel that this is my city; I own a part of this Capital, and I envy for the time being those who are able to spend their time here. I quite admit that there are defects in the system of government by which Congress is bound to look after the government of the District of Columbia. It could not be otherwise under such a system, but I submit to the judgment of history that the result vindicates the foresight of the fathers."

"Anti-Semitism is a noxious weed that should be cut out. It has no place in America."

"Enthusiasm for a cause sometimes warps judgment."

"If this humor be the safety of our race, then it is due largely to the infusion into the American people of the Irish brain."

"Failure to accord credit to anyone for what he may have done is a great weakness in any man."

"I think I might as well give up being a candidate. There are so many people in the country who don't like me."

28. WOODROW WILSON (1913-1921)

"Sometimes people call me an idealist. Well, that is the way I know am an American. America is the only idealistic nation in the world."

"America lives in the heart of every man everywhere who wishes to find a region where he will be free to work out his destiny as he chooses."

"We grow great by dreams. All big men the dreamers."

"The things that the flag stands for created by the experience of a great people. Everything that it stands for was written by their lives. The flag is the embodiment, not of sentiment, but of history."

"Democracy is not so much a form of government as a set of principles."

"When I gave a man an office, I watch him carefully to see whether he is swelling or growing."

"If you want to make enemies, try to change something."

"If you think too much about being re-elected, it is very difficult to be worth re-electing."

"The Constitution was not made to fit us like a straitjacket. In its elasticity lies its chief greatness."

"I used to be a lawyer, but now I am a reformed character."

"America is nothing if it consists of each of us. It is something only if it consists of all of us."

"Hunger does not breed reform, it breeds madness, and all the ugly distempers that make an order life impossible."

"I not only use all of the brains I have, but all I can borrow."

"Life does not consist in thinking, it consists in acting."

"I would rather belong to a poor nation that was free than to a rich nation that had ceased to be in love with liberty."

"I believe in democracy because it releases the energies of every human being."

"No man that does not see visions will ever realize any high hope or undertake any high enterprise."

"One cool judgment is worth a thousand hasty councils. The thing to do is to supply light and not heat."

"Only free peoples can hold their purpose and their honor steady to a common end and prefer the interest of mankind to any narrow interest of their own."

"Liberty has never come from government. Liberty has always come from the subjects of government. The history of liberty of resistance. The history of liberty is a history of the limitation of governmental power not the increase of it."

"Freedom exists only where the people take care of the government."

"Provision for others is a fundamental responsibility of human life."

"There must be, not a balance of power, but a community of power, not organized rivalries, but an organization of common peace."

"Liberty has never come from the government. Liberty has always come from the subjects of it. The history of liberty is a history of resistance."

"Liberty is its own reward."

"Big business is not dangerous because it is big, but because its bigness is an unwholesome inflation created by privileges and exemptions which it ought not to enjoy."

"There is a power somewhere so organized, so subtle, so watchful, so interlocked, so pervasive that they better not speak above their breath when they speak in condemnation of it."

"The individual is indisputable the original, the first fact of liberty…There is no such thing as corporate liberty. Liberty belongs to the individual, or it does not exist."

"The man who is swimming against the stream knows the strength of it."

"The sum of the whole matter is this – our civilization cannot survive materially unless it be redeemed spirituality."

"You are not here merely to make a living. You are here in order to enable the world to live more amply, with greater vision, with a finer spirit of hope and achievement. You are here to enrich the world, and you impoverish yourself if you forget the errand."

"In the Lord's Prayer, the first petition is for daily bread. No one can worship God or love his neighbor on an empty stomach."

29. WILLIAM G. HARDING (1921-1923)

"America's present need is not heroics, but healing; not nostrums, but normalcy; not revolution, but restoration; not agitation, but adjustment; not surgery, but serenity; not the dramatic, but the dispassionate; not experiment, nut equipoise; not submergence in internationally, but sustainment in triumphant nationality..."

"I don't know much about Americanism, but it's a damn good word with which to carry an election."

"There is something inherently wrong, something out of accord with the ideals of representative democracy, when one portion of our citizenship turns its activities to private gain amid defensive war while another is fighting, sacrificing, or dying for national preservation."

"Our most dangerous tendency is to expect too much of government, and at the same time do for it too little."

"In the great fulfillment we must have a citizenship less concerned about what the government can do for it and more anxious about what it can do for the nation."

"I don't know what to do or where to turn in this taxation matter. Somewhere there must be a book that tells all about it, where I could go to straighten it out in my mind. But I don't know where the book is, and maybe I couldn't read it if I found it."

"Ours is not only a fortunate people but a very common sensical people, with vision high but their feet on the earth, with belief in themselves and faith in God."

"The success of our popular government rests wholly upon the correct interpretation of the deliberate, intelligent, dependable popular will of America."

"My God, this is a hell of a job! I have no trouble with my enemies ... but my damn friends, they're the ones that keep me walking the floor nights!"

"Ambition is a commendable attribute without which no man succeeds. Only inconsiderate ambition imperils."

"Only solitary man knows the full joys of friendship. Others have their family, but to a solitary man and an exile, his friends are everything."

"I have no trouble with my enemies. I can take care of my enemies in a fight. But my friends, my goddamned friends, they're the ones who keep me walking the floor at night!"

"It is my conviction that the fundamental trouble with the people of the United States that they have gotten too far away from Almighty God."

30. CALVIN COOLIDGE (1923-1929)

"In the discharge of the duties of this office, there is one rule of action more important than all others. It consists in never doing anything that someone else can do for you."

"Liberty is not collective, it is personal. All liberty is individual liberty."

(Speech, 1924)

I have found it advisable not to give too much heed to what people say when I am trying to accomplish something of consequence. Invariably they proclaim it can't be done. I deem that the very best time to make the effort."

"The business of America is business."

"No matter what anyone may say about making the rich and the corporations pay taxes, in the end they come out of the people who toil."

"When large numbers of men are unable to find work, unemployment results."

"Collecting more taxes than is absolutely necessary is legalized robbery."

"No man ever listened himself out of a job."

"It takes a great man to be a good listener."

"Never go out to meet trouble. If you will just sit still, nine cases out of ten someone will intercept it before it reaches you."

"Knowledge comes, but wisdom lingers. It may not be difficult to store up in the mind a vast quantity of face within a comparatively short time, but the ability to form judgments requires the severe discipline of hard work and the tempering heat of experience and maturity."

"Prosperity is only an instrument to be used, not a deity to be worshipped."

"All growth depends upon activity. There is no development physically or intellectually without effort, and effort means work."

"Nothing in the world can take the place of Persistence. Talent will not; nothing is more common than unsuccessful men with talent. Genius will not; unrewarded genius is almost a proverb. Education will not; the world is full of educated derelicts. Persistence and determination alone are omnipotent. The slogan 'Press On' has solved and always will solve the problems of the human race."

"If I has permitted my failures, or what seemed to me at the time a lack of success, to discourage me I cannot see any way in which I would ever have made progress."

"We do not need more intellectual power, we need more spiritual power. We do not need more of the things that are seen, we need more of the things that are unseen."

"Borrowed money, even when owing to a nation by another nation, should be repaid."

"Christmas is not a time nor a season, but a state of mind. To cherish peace and goodwill, to be plenteous in mercy, is to have the real spirit if Christmas."

"One with the law is a majority."

"A nation which forgets its defenders will be itself forgotten."

"Those who trust to chance must abide by the results of chance."

"It is the duty of a citizen not only to observe the law, but to let it be known that he is opposed to its violation."

"There is no force so democratic as the force of an ideal."

"Men speak of natural rights, but I challenge anyone to show where in nature any rights existed or were recognized until there was established for their declaration and protection a duly promulgated body of corresponding laws."

"Men do not make laws. They do but discover them. Laws must be justified by something more than the will of the majority. They must rest on the eternal foundation of righteousness. That state is the most fortunate which has the aptest instruments for the discovery of laws."

"It is only when men begin to worship that they begin to grow."

"Our doctrine of equality and liberty and humanity comes from our belief in the brotherhood of man, through the fatherhood of God."

"Perhaps one of the most important accomplishments of my administration has been minding my own business."

"I have never been hurt by anything I didn't say."

"If you don't say anything, you won't be called upon to repeat it."

"The right thing to do never requires any subterfuge, it is always simple and direct."

"Character is the only secure foundation of the state."

"The chief business of the American people is business."

"No person was ever honored for what he received. Honor has been the reward for what he gave."

"There is no right to strike against the public safety by anybody, anywhere, anytime."

"It would be folly to argue that the people cannot make political mistakes. They can and do make grave mistakes. They know it, they pay the penalty, but compared with the mistakes that have been made by every kind of autocracy, they are unimportant."

"Patriotism is easy to understand in America. It means looking out for yourself by looking out for your country."

"To live the American Constitution is the greatest political privilege that was ever accorded to the human race."

"I have found it advisable not to give too much heed to what people say when I am trying to accomplish something of consequence. Invariably they proclaim it can't be done. I deem that they very best time to make the effort."

"Don't expect to build up the weak by pulling down the strong."

"Nothing in the world can take the place of persistence. Talent will not; nothing is more common than unsuccessful men with talent. Genius will not; unrewarded genius is almost a proverb. Education will not; the world is full of educated derelicts. Persistence and determination are omnipotent. The slogan "press on" has solved and always will solve the problems of the human race.

"Heroism is not only in the man, but in the occasion."

"We draw our Presidents from the people. It is a wholesome thing for them to return to the people. I came from them. I wish to be one of them again."

31. HERBERT C. HOOVER (1929-1933)

"Freedom is the open window through which pours the sunlight of the human spirit and human dignity."

"My country owes me nothing. It gave me, as it gives every boy and girl, a chance. It gave me schooling, independence of action, opportunity for service and honor. In no other land could a boy from a country village, without inheritance or influential friends, look forward with unbounded hope."

"Economic freedom cannot be sacrificed if political freedom is to be preserved."

"Absolute freedom of the press to discuss public questions is a foundation stone of American liberty."

"A splendid storehouse of integrity and freedom has been bequeathed to us by our forefathers. In this day of confusion, of peril to liberty, our high duty is to see that this storehouse is not robbed of its contents."

"True Liberalism is found not in striving to spread bureaucracy but in striving to set bounds to it."

"Above all, we know that although Americans can be led to make great sacrifices, they do not like to be driven."

"When there is a lack o honor in government, the morals of the whole people are poisoned."

"In the great mass of our people there are plenty individuals of intelligence from among whom leadership can be recruited."

"Wisdom consists not so much in knowing what to do in the ultimate as in knowing what to do next."

"Blessed are the young, for they will inherit the national debt."

"I'm the only person of distinction who's ever had a depression named for him."

"There are only two occasions when Americans respect privacy, especially from Presidents. Those are prayer and fishing."

"Peace is not made at the Council table or by treaties, but in the hearts of men."

"A splendid storehouse of integrity and freedom has been bequeathed to us by our forefathers. In this day of confusion, of peril to liberty, our high duty is to see that this storehouse is not robbed of its contents."

"Absolute freedom pf the press to discuss public questions is a foundation stone of American history."

"Older men declare war. But it is the youth that must fight and die."

"Children are out most valuable natural resource."

"Hunger is the mother of anarchy."

"No greater nor more affectionate honor can be conferred on an American than to have a public school named after him"

"Every president should have the right to two reporter's a year— without explanation."

"Equality of opportunity is the right of every American—rich or poor, foreign or native-born, irrespective of faith or color... Only form confidence that this right will be upheld can flow that unbounded courage and hope which stimulate each individual man and woman to endeavor and to achievement. The sum of their achievement is the gigantic harvest of national progress."

"Words without actions are the assassins of idealism."

"About the time we can make ends meet, somebody moves the ends."

32. FRANKLIN DELANO ROOSEVELT (1933-1945)

"The United States Constitution has proved itself the most marvelously elastic compilation of rules of government ever written."

"We must especially beware of that small group of selfish men who would clip the wings of the American eagle in order to feather their own nests."

"No democracy can long survive which does not accept as fundamental to its very existence the recognition of the rights of minorities."

"The Presidency is not merely an administrative office. That's the least of it. It is more than an engineering job, efficient or inefficient. It is preeminently a place of moral leadership."

"Yesterday, December 7, 1941 – a date that will live in infamy – the United States of America was suddenly and deliberately attacked by naval and air forces of the Empire of Japan."

"We can see now that we Americans were caught unprepared. Because we were ordinary human beings, following the best advice we had at the time. No one would have guessed in 1941 that we would be attacked in such an unsportsmanlike manner as we were. No one could have visualized Pearl Harbor, either out there or in Washington. But if we had known then what we know now, we would have expected an attack in 1941."

"We, and all others who believe in freedom as deeply as we do, would rather die on our feet than live on our knees."

"But while they prate of economic laws, men and women are starving. We must lay hold of the fact that economic laws are not made by nature. They are made by human beings."

"The test of our progress is not whether we add more to the abundance of those who have much; it is whether we provide enough for those who have too little."

"Peace, like charity, begins at home."

"The only thing we have to fear is fear itself."

"The only limit to our realization of tomorrow will be our doubts of today; let us move forward with strong and active faith."

"It is the duty of the President to propose and it is the privilege of the Congress to dispose."

"There is a mysterious cycle in human events. To some generations much is given. Of other generations much is expected."

"A good leader can't get too far ahead of his followers."

"Happiness lies in the joy of achievement and the thrill of creative effort."

"When you see a rattlesnake poised to strike, you do not wait until he has struck before your crush him."

"Human kindness has never weakened the stamina or softened the fiber of a free people."

"We are a nation of many nationalities, many races, many religions—bound together by a single unity, the unity of freedom and equality. Whoever seeks to set one nationality against another seeks to degrade all nationalities."

"We must remember that any oppression, any injustice, any hatred, is a wedge designed to attack our civilization."

"We, too, born in freedom, and believing in freedom are willing to fight to maintain freedom. We, and all others who believe as deeply as we do, would rather die on our feet than live on our knees."

"The country needs and, unless I mistake its temper, the country demands bold, persistent experimentation. It is common sense to take a method and try it; if it fails, admit it frankly and try another. But, above all, try."

"True individual freedom cannot exist without economic security and independence. People who are hungry and out of a job are the stuff of which dictatorships are made of."

"In the truest sense, freedom cannot be bestowed; it must be achieved."

"Four Freedoms"

The first is freedom of speech and expression...everywhere in the world.

The Second is freedom of everyone to worship God in his own way... everywhere in the world.

The Third is freedom from want...everywhere in the world.

The Fourth is freedom from fear...everywhere in the world.

(The Four Freedom, Speech, January 6, 1941)

"If in other lands the press and books and literature of all kinds are censored, we must redouble our efforts here to keep them free."

"Those who have long enjoyed such privileges as we enjoy forget in time that men have died to win them."

"The only limit to our realization of tomorrow will be our doubts of today. Let us move forward with strong and active faith."

"Nothing is so responsible for the good old days as a bad memory."

"Human kindness has never weakened the stamina or softened fiber of a free people. A nation does not have to be cruel in order to be tough."

"We are a nation of many nationalities, many races, many religions—bound together by a single unity, the unity of freedom and equality. Whoever seeks to set one nationality against another, seeks to degrade all nationalities."

"A man who has never gone to school may steal from a freight car, but if he has a university education he may steal the whole railroad."

"It is common sense to take a method and try it. If all fails, admit it frankly and try another. But above all, try something."

"Men are not prisoners of fate, but only prisoners of their own mind."

"No man is justified in doing evil on the ground of expedience."

"The ablest man I ever met is the man you think you are."

"We cannot always build the future for our youth, but we can build our youth for the future."

"When you get to the end of your rope, tie a knot and hang on."

33. HARRY S. TRUMAN (1945-1953)

"When you get to be President, there are all those thing, the honors, the twenty-one gun salutes, all those things. You have to remember it isn't for you. It's for the Presidency."

"Washington is a very easy city for you to forget where you came from and why you got there in the first place."

"A politician is a man who understands government and it takes a politician to run a government. A statesman is a politician who's been dead ten or fifteen years."

"Within the first few months, I discovered that being a President is like riding a tiger. A man has to keep on riding or be swallowed."

"Peace is the goal of my life. I'd rather have lasting peace in the world than be President. I wish for peace, I work for peace and I pray for peace continually."

"My father was not a failure. After all. He was the father of a President of the United States."

"You can not stop the spread of an idea by passing a law against it."

"Most of the problems a president has to face have their roots in the past."

"If we falter in our leadership we may endanger the peace of he world, and we hall surely endanger the welfare of the nation."

"Leadership is the ability to get people to do what they don't want to do and like it."

"Any man who has had the job I've had and didn't have a sense of humor wouldn't still be here."

"Racial and religious oppression – big business domination – inflation – these forces must be stopped and driven back while there is yet time."

"Without…advertising, information…would take years to reach all of us who might benefit by it and progress would be delayed."

America was not built on fear. America was built on courage, on imagination and unbeatable determination to do the job at hand." (January 8, 1947)

"All the president is, is a glorified public relations man who spends his time flattering, kissing, and kicking people to get them to do what they are supposed to do anyway."

"The basis for our Bill of Rights comes from the teachings we get from Exodus and St. Matthew, from Isaiah and St. Paul. I don't think we can emphasize that enough these days. If we don't have a proper founded moral background, we will finally end up with a government, which does not believe in rights for anybody except the state."

"The Bill of Rights, contained in the first ten amendments to the Constitution, is every American's guarantee of freedom."

"The seeds of totalitarian regimes are nurtured by misery and want. They spread and grow in the evil soil of poverty and strife. They reach their full growth when the hop of a people for a better life has died. We must keep hope alive." ('The Truman Doctrine' – March 12, 1947)

"I don't like bi-partisans. Whenever a fellow tells me he's bi-partisan, I know that he's going to vote against me." (January 21, 1962)

"When you have an efficient government, you have a dictatorship."

"The only thing new in the world is the history you don't know."

"We should resolve now that the health of the nation is a national concern; that financial barriers in the way of attaining health shall be removed; that the health of all its citizens deserves the help of all the nation."

"We must have strong minds, ready to accept facts as they are."

"Always be sincere even if you don't mean it."

"When even one American – who has done nothing wrong – is forced by fear to shut his min and close his mouth, then all Americans are in peril."

"Whenever you put a man on the Supreme Court, he ceases to be your friend."

"He (Zachary Taylor) became an expert at doing nothing." (More Plain Speaking)

"We must remember that the test f our religious principles lies not just in what we say, not only in our prayers not even in living blameless lives – but in what we do for others." (January 28, 1951)

"When even one American – who has done nothing wrong – is forced by fear to shut his mind and close his mouth, then all of Americans are in peril."

"Intense feeling too often obscures the truth." (Speech, October 19, 1948)

"I never sit on a fence. I am either on one side or another." (Speech, October 30, 1948)

"About the meanest thing you can say about a man is that he means well." (Speech, May 10, 1950)

"The Republicans believe that the power of government should be used fist of all to help the rich and the privileged in the country. With them, property, wealth, comes first. The Democrats believe that the power of government should be used to give the common man more protection and a chance to make a living. With us the people come first. (A Government as Good As Its People – pg 163)

"Study men, not historians."

"I suppose that history will remember my term in office as the years when the Cold War began to overshadow our lives. I have hardly a day in office that has not been dominated by this all-embracing struggle. And always in the background there has been the atomic bomb. But when history says that my term of office saw the beginning of the Cold War, it will also say that in those eight years we have set the course that can win it."

"Richard Nixon is a no good, lying bastard. He can lie out of both sides of his mouth at the same time, and if he ever caught himself telling the truth, he'd lie just to keep his hand in"

"It is futile to seek safety beyond geographical barriers. Real security will be found only in the law and in justice." (Addressing the nation upon the death of FDR)

"It's a lot better to have a strong national defense than a balanced budget." (February 17, 1957)

"You can always amend a big plan, but you can never expand a little one. I don't believe in little plans. I believe in plans big enough to meet a situation which we can't possibly foresee now."

"To me, party platforms are contracts with the people."

"Men make history, and not the other way around. In periods where there is no leadership, society stands still. Progress occurs when courageous, skillful leaders seize the opportunity to change things for the better."

"It isn't important who is ahead at one time or another in either an election or horse race. It's the horse that comes in first at the finish line that counts." (1948)

"We must build a new world, a far better world – one in which the eternal dignity of man is respected."

"The nation's labor force is its most productive asset."

"A person who is fundamentally honest doesn't need a cod of ethics. The Ten Commandments and the Sermon on the Mount are all the ethical codes anybody needs." (Remarks, July 10, 1958)

"It's a recession when your neighbor loses his job, it's a depression when you lose your own."

"It is not the martinets that make an army work; it's the morals that the leaders put into the men that makes an army work." (Speech October 24, 1950)

"When you have to deal with a beast, you have to treat him as a beast. It is most regrettable but nevertheless true."

"It's not the hand that signs the laws that holds the destiny of America. It's the hand that casts the ballot."

"I never gave them hell, I just tell the truth and they think its hell."

"Carry the battle to them. Don't let them bring it to you. Put them on the defensive. And don't ever apologize to anyone."

"I have found the best way to give advice to your children is to find out what they want and then advise them to do it."

"Our allies are the millions who hunger and thirst after righteousness." (July 6, 1947)

"We need not fear the expression of ideas-we do need to fear their suppression."

"A pessimist is one who makes difficulties of his opportunities and an optimist is one who makes opportunities of his difficulties."

"It is amazing what you can accomplish if you do not care who gets the credit."

"It's a recession when your neighbor losses his job; it's a depression when you lose yours."

"I never give them hell. I just tell the truth and they think it is hell."

"I'm proud that I'm a politician. A politician is a man who understands government, and it take a politician to run a government. A statesman is a politician who's been dead 10 to 15 years."

"When a fellow tells me he's bipartisan, I know he's going to vote against me."

"Whenever you have an efficient government you have a dictatorship."

"America was not built on fear. America was built on courage, on imagination, and unbeatable determination to do the job at hand."

"We believe that all men are created equal because they are created in the image of God."

"When even one American – who has done nothing wrong – is forced by fear to shut his mind and close his mouth, then all Americans are in peril."

"If you can' beat them, confuse them."

"It is amazing what you can accomplish if you do not care w gets the credit."

"All my life, whenever it comes time to make a decision make it and forget about it."

"Secrecy and a free, democratic government don't mix."

"If you can't stand the heat, get out of the kitchen."

"Some of the Presidents were great and some of them weren't. I can say that, because I wasn't one of the great Presidents, but I had a good time trying to be one, I can tell you that."

34. DWIGHT D. EISENHOWER (1953-1961)

"America is best described by one word, freedom."

"I never saw a pessimistic general win a battle."

"There is nothing wrong with America that the faith, love of freedom, intelligence and energy of her citizens cannot cure."

"Whatever America hopes to bring to pass in the world must first come to pass in the heart of America."

"Only our individual faith in freedom can keep us free."

"Our American heritage is threatened as much by our own indifference as by the most unscrupulous office or by the most powerful foreign threat. The future of this republic is in the hands of the American voter."

"There is one thing about being President—nobody can tell you when to sit down."

"No easy problems ever come to the President of the United States. If they are easy to solve, somebody else has solved them."

"I can think of nothing more boring for the American people than to have to sit in their living rooms for a whole half hour looking at my face on their television screens."

"Americans, indeed all free men, remember that in the final choice, a soldier's pack is not so heavy a burden as a prisoner's chains."

"Though force can protect in emergency, only justice, fairness, consideration and co-operation can finally lead men to the dawn of eternal peace."

"I like to believe that people in the long run are going to do more to promote peace than our governments. Indeed, I think that people want peace so much that one of these days governments had better get out of the way and let them have it."

"A people that values its privileges above its principles, soon loses both." (January 20, 1953)

"Don't ever become a general. If you become a general, you just plain have too much to worry about." (The Toastmaster's Treasure Chest)

"Anytime we deny any citizen the full exercise of his constitutional rights, we are weakening our own claim to them." (Reader's Digest, December 1963)

"What counts is not necessarily the size of the dog in the fight – it's the size of the fight in the dog."

"Finally, you have broader considerations that might follow what you would call the "falling domino" principle. You have a row of dominoes set up, you knock over the first one, and what will happen to the last one is the certainly that it will go over very quickly. So you could have a beginning of a disintegration that would have the most profound influences."

"Among these treasures of our land is water—fast becoming our most valuable, most prized, most critical resource. A blessing where properly used—but it can bring devastation and ruin when left uncontrolled.

"Before all else, we seek, upon our common labor as a nation, the blessings of Almighty God."

"A sense of humor is part of the art of leadership. Of getting along with people, of getting things done."

"Things are more like they are now than they ever were before."

"Like all successful politicians I married above myself."

"People talk about the middle of the road as though it were unacceptable. Actually, all human problems, excepting morals, come into the gray areas. Things are not all black and white. There have to be compromises. The middle of the road is all of the usable surface. The extremes, right and left, are in the gutters."

"Politics is a profession, a serious, complicated and, in its true sense, a noble one."

"Politics ought to be the part-time profession of every citizen who would protect the rights and privileges of free people and who would preserve what is good and fruitful in ournational heritage. (January 1954

"The future of this republic is in the hands of the American voter."

"Though force can protect in emergency, only justice, fairness, consideration and cooperation can finally lead men to the dawn of eternal peace."

"We seek peace, knowing that peace is the climate of freedom."

"When you are in any contest you should work as if there were – to the very last minute – a chance to lose it."

"If you want total security, go to prison. There you're fed, clothed, given medical care and so on. The only thing lacking…is Freedom."

"History does not long entrust the care of freedom to the weak or the timid."

"I think that people want peace so much that one of these days government had better get out of their way and let them have it."

"An intellectual is a man who takes more words than necessary to tell more than he knows."

"Don't think you are going to conceal thoughts by concealing evidence that they ever existed."

"When you are in any contest you should work as if there were – to the very last minute – a chance to lose it."

"We succeed only as we identify in life, or in war, or in anything else, a single over-riding objective, and make all other considerations bend to that one objective." (Speech, April 2, 1957)

35. JOHN F. KENNEDY (1961 – 1963)

"The Constitution makes us not rivals for power but partners for progress." (State of the Union, 1962)

"In politics, there are no friends, only allies."

"Liberty without learning is always in peril and learning without liberty is always in vain."

"I have just received the following telegram from my generous daddy. It says 'Dear Jack: Don't buy a single vote more than necessary. I'll be damned if I'm going to pay for a landslide." (Gridiron Dinner, Washington, DC, 1958)

"We stand today on the edge of a New Frontier. The New Frontier of which I speak is not a set of promises—it is a set of challenges. It sums up not what I intend to offer the American people, but what I intend to ask of them…It appeals to our pride, not our security—it holds the promise of more sacrifice instead of more security." (Acceptance speech, July 15, 1960)

"It has recently been suggested that whether I serve one or two terms in the Presidency, I will find myself at the end of that period at what night be called the awkward age, too old to begin a new career and too young to write my memoirs." (February 12, 1961)

"I think this is the most extraordinary collection of talent, of human knowledge, that has ever been gathered together at the White House—with the possible exception of when Thomas Jefferson dined alone." (April 29, 1962)

"It is time for a new generation of leadership, to cope with new problems and new opportunities. For there is a new world to be run."

"All this will not be finished in the first 100 days. Nor will it be finished in the first 1,000 days, not in the life of this Administration, nor even perhaps in our lifetime on this planet. But, let us begin."

"I don't see what's wrong with giving Bobby a little experience before he starts to practice law." (John F. Kennedy, appointing his brother Bobby, US Attorney General)

"Only a respect for the law makes it possible for free men to dwell together in peace and progress…Law is the adhesive force in the cement of society, creating order out of chaos and coherence in place of anarchy." (May 18, 1963)

"We are not afraid to entrust the American people with unpleasant facts, foreign ideas, alien philosophies, and competitive values. For a nation that is afraid to let its people judge the truth and falsehood in an open market is a nation that is afraid of its people."

"Every American ought to have the right to b treated; as he would like to be treated, as one would wish to be treated, as one would wish his children to be treated."

"I look forward to an America which commands respect throughout the world, not only for its strength, but for its civilization as well. And I look forward to a world which will be safe not only for democracy and diversity but also for personal distinction." (October 6, 1963 Amherst College)

"The stories of past courage can define that ingredient—they can teach, they can offer hope, they can provide inspiration. But they cannot supply courage itself. For this each man must look into his own soul."

"The American, by nature, is optimistic. He is experimental, an inventor and a builder who builds best when called upon to build greatly."

"A nation reveals itself not only by the men it produces but also by the men it honors, the men it remembers."

"Great crises produce great men, and great deeds of courage."

"A man may die, nations may rise and fall, but an idea lives on."

"Change is the law of life. And those who look only to the past or present are certain to miss the future."

"We must never forget that art is not a form of propaganda; it is a form of truth." (October 26, 1963)

"A man does what he must – in spite of personal consequences, in spite of obstacles and dangers – and this is the basis of all human morality."

"Peace is a daily, a weekly, a monthly process, gradually changing opinions, slowly eroding old barriers, quietly building new structures."

"So let us preserver. Peace need not be impracticable—and war need not be inevitable. By defining our goal more clearly, by making it seem more manageable and less remote, we can help all peoples to see it, to draw hope from it, and to move irresistibly towards it." (1963)

"Peace and freedom walk together. In too many of our cities today, the peace is not secure because freedom is incomplete." (June 10, 1963)

"The best road to progress is freedom's road."

"The time to repair the roof is when the sun is shining."

"History will never accept difficulties as an excuse."

"Forgive your enemies, but never forget their names."

"Conformity is the jailer of freedom and the enemy of growth." (Speech to the United Nations, 1961)

"Man is still the most extraordinary computer of all."

"A child miseducated is a child lost."

"Efforts and courage are not enough without purpose and direction."

"Any dangerous spot is tenable if rave men will make it so."

"Do you know the responsibility I carry I'm the only person between Nixon and the White House."

"Let us never negotiate out of fear, but let us never fear to negotiate."

"Mr. Nixon, in the last seven days, has called me an economic ignoramus, a Pied Piper, and all the rest. I have just confined myself o calling him a Republican, but he says that is getting low." (November 5, 1960)

"[Mr. President, how did you become a war hero?] It was absolutely involuntary. They sank my boat." (The Kennedy Wit)

"My brother Bob doesn't want to be in government—he promised Dad he'd go straight."

"Our problems are man-made, therefore, they may be solved by man. No problem of human destiny is beyond human beings."

"If a free society cannot help the many who are poor, it cannot save the few who are rich." (January 20, 1963)

"Our restraint is not inexhaustible." (April 20, 1961)

"The quality of American life must keep pace with the quantity of American goods. This country cannot afford to be materially rich and spiritually poor."

"There are three things in life which are real: God, human folly and laughter. Since the first two are beyond our comprehension, we must do what we can with the third."

"We have come too far,we have sacrificed too much, to disdain the future now."

"The Constitution makes us not rivals for power but partners for progress."

"In each of us, there is a private hope and dream which, fulfilled, can be translated into benefit for everyone."

"In a time of turbulence and change, it is more true today than ever that knowledge is power."

"We shall be judged more by what we do at home than what we preached abroad." (State of the Union, 1963)

"Let us never negotiate out of fear but let us never fear to negotiate." (January 20, 1961)

"With a good conscience our only sure reward, with history the final judge of our deeds, let us go forth to lead the land we love."

"The American farmer is the only man in our economy who buy everything he buys at retail, sells everything he sells at wholesale, and pays the freight both ways." (September 22, 1960)

"This nation was founded by men of many nations and backgrounds. It was founded on the principle that all men are created equal and that the rights of every man are diminished when the rights of one man are threatened." (June 11, 1963)

"It might be said now that I have the best of both worlds: a Harvard education and a Yale degree." (Accepting a Yale degree, June 12, 1963)

"Today, we need a nation of Minutemen, citizens who are not only prepared to take arms, but citizens who regard the preservation of freedom as the basic purpose of their daily life and who are willing to consciously work and sacrifice for that freedom."

"We cannot expect that all nations will adopt like systems, for conformity is the jailer of freedom and the enemy of growth."

"And so my fellow Americans, ask not what your country can do for you; ask what you can do for your country. My fellow citizens of the world: ask not what America will do for you, but together we can do for the freedom of man."

"The world is a very different now…and yet the same revolutionary beliefs for which our forebears fought are still at issue around the globe—the belief that the rights of man come not from the generosity of the state but from the hand of God."

"If we cannot end now our differences, at least, we can help make the world safe for diversity."

"Victory has a thousand fathers, but defeat is an orphan."

"Let every nation know, whether it wishes use well or ill, that we shall pay any price, bear any burden, meet any hardship, support any friend, oppose any foe to assure the survival and success of liberty."

"In the long history of the world, only a few generations have been granted the role of defending freedom in its hour of maximum danger. I do not shrink from this responsibility— I welcome it."

"In the past, these who foolishly sought power by riding on the back of the tiger ended up inside."

"My experience in government is that when things are non-controversial and beautifully coordinated, there is not much going on."

"Now the trumpet summons us again—not as a call to bear arms; though arms we need—not as a call to battle, though embattled we are—but a call to bear the burden of a long twilight struggle year in and year out, "rejoicing in hope, patient in tribulation"—a struggle against the common enemies of man: tyranny, poverty and war itself."

"Our progress as a nation can be no swifter than our progress in education."

"The cost of freedom is always high, but Americans have always paid it. And one path we shall never choose, and that is the path of surrender, or submission."

"The efforts of the government alone will never be enough, on the end the people must choose and the people must help themselves."

"The great enemy of the truth is very often not the lie—deliberate, contrived, and dishonest—but the myth—persistent, persuasive, and unrealistic."

"The margin is narrow, but the responsibility is clear."

"You know nothing for sure...except the fact that you know nothing for sure."

"Mothers all want their sons to grow up to be president, but they don't want them to become politicians in the process."

"The political world is stimulating. It's the most interesting thing you can do. It beats following the dollar."

"The unity of freedom has never relied on uniformity of opinion."

"We have the power to make this the best generation of mankind in the history of the world—or the last."

"…that government of the people, by the people, for the people shall not perish from earth."

"Let us resolve to be masters, not the victims, of our history, controlling our own blind suspicious and emotions."

"I am certain that after the dust of centuries has passed over our cities, we, too, victories or defeats in battle or in politics, but for our contributions."

"Mankind must put an end to war, or war will put an end to mankind."

"All this will not be finished in the first one hundred days. Nor will it be finished in the first thousand days, nor in the life of this administration, nor even perhaps in our lifetime on this planet. So, let us begin."

"The courage of life is often a less dramatic spectacle than the courage of the final moment' but it is no less a magnificent mixture of triumph and tragedy."

"We are not against any man – or any nation – or any system – except as it is hostile to freedom."

"If we are strong, our strength will speak for itself."

"Liberty without learning is always in peril and learning without liberty is always in vain."

"It may be different elsewhere. But a democratic society – in it, the highest duty of the writer, the composer and the artist is to remain true to himself and to let the chips fall where they may."

"If a free society cannot help the many who are poor, it cannot save the few who are rich."

"If men and women are in chains anywhere in the world, then freedom is endangered everywhere."

"I am certain that after the dust of the centuries has passed over our cities, we too, will be remembered not for our victories or defeat in battle or in politics, but for our contributions to the human spirit."

"This nation has tossed its cap over the wall of space, and we have no choice but to follow it." (President John F. Kennedy, Remarks at the dedication of the Aerospace Medical Health Center, San Antonio, Texas, November 21, 1963, a day before he was assassinated in Dallas, Texas, November 22, 1963)

36. LYNDON BAINES JOHNSON (1963-1969)

"I will do my best. That is all I can do. I ask for your help, and God's... (After President John F. Kennedy's Death)

"A President's hardest task is not to do what is right, but to do what is right, but to know what is right."

"Words wound. But as a veteran of twelve years in the United States Senate, I happily attest that they do not kill." (Speech, Denver, August 26, 1966)

"The presidency is not just a place to protect the present. It is a focus for the possibilities of the future."

"For every generation, there is a destiny. For some, history decides. For this generation, the choice must be our own." President Lyndon Johnson in his inaugural address.)

"I am the only President you've got." (Reminder to US Senators, April 27, 1964)

"If we must disagree, let's disagree without being disagreeable." (Remarks to US Senators, 1965)

"You're asking the leader of the Western world a chicken shit question like that?

"Lincoln was right about not fooling all the people all the time. But, Republicans haven't given up trying.

"A man increases his knowledge of the heavens, why should he fear the unknown on earth? As man draws nearer to the stars, why should he not also draw nearer to his neighbor?

"My White House job pays more than public school systems but the tenure is less certain."

"Education is not a problem. Education is an opportunity."

"...I have called for a national war on poverty. Our objective: total victory."

"It is not enough just to open the gates of opportunity. All our citizens must have the ability to walk through those gates. This is the next, and the most profound stage of the battle for civil rights." (Signing the Clean Water Act of 1965)

"Jerry Ford is so stupid he couldn't chew gum and crap at the same time."

"Our fate as a nation and our future as a people rest not upon one citizen, but upon citizens."

"We all have differences. Men of different ancestries, men of different tongues, men of different colors, men of different environments, men of different geographies, do not see everything a like. If we did, we would all want the same wife—and that would be a problem. Wouldn't it?" (Speech, February 11, 1964)

"The Great Society is a place where every child can find knowledge to enrich his mind and to enlarge his talents... It is a place where the city of man serves not only the needs of the body and the demands of commerce but the desire for beauty and the hunger for community....It is a place where men are more concerned with the quality of their goals than the quantity of their goods."

"The Mother Hubbard speech which, like the garment. Covers everything but touches nothing; and he French bathing suit speech which covers only the essential points." (The Johnson Humor)

"There are not problems we cannot solve together, and very few we can solve by ourselves." Speech at the NATO Alliance, 1964)

"You fellows know what a steer is. That's a bull who's lost his social standing." (The Johnson Humor)

"The art of preserving peace is greater than that of waging war, and much more demanding."

"This, then, is the state of the union, free and restless, growing and full of hope. So, it was in the beginning. So, it shall always be, while God is willing, and we are strong enough to keep the faith."

"You ain't learnin' nothin' when you're talkin'."

"For this is what America is all about. It is the uncrossed desert and the unclimbed ridge. It is the star that is not reached and the harvest sleeping in the unplowed ground ..."

"Men who have worked together to reach the stars are not likely to descend together into the depths of war and desolation."

"He (Barry Goldwater) wants to repeal the present and veto the future." (The Johnson Humor, Bill Adler)

"The people of the United States love and voted for Harry Truman, not because he gave them hell—but because he gave them hope."

"Better to have him inside the tent pissing out, than outside pissing in." (On J. Edgar Hoover, Head of the FBI)

"I want real loyalty. I want someone who will kiss my ass in Macy's window, and say it smells like roses."

"I'm a compromiser and a maneuver, I try to get something. That's the way our system work. (NY Times, December 8, 1963)

"If government is to serve any purpose it is to do for others what they are unable to do for themselves."

"The noblest search is the search for excellence."

"If one morning I walked on top of the water across the Potomac River, the headline that afternoon would read "President Can't Swim.""

"I never think of politics more than eighteen hours a day." The Johnson Humor)

"Conservation is ethically sound. It is rooted in our love of the land, our respect for the rights of others, our devotion to the rule of law."

"Doing what's right isn't the problem. It's knowing what's right."

"If there is one word that describes our form of society in America, it may be the world voluntary."

"The world has narrowed to a neighborhood before it has broadened to brotherhood."

"If we are to live together in peace, we must come to know each other better."

"Yesterday is not ours to recover, but tomorrow is ours to win or lose."

"American people have a right to air that they and their children can breathe without fear."

"The hungry world cannot be fed until and unless the growth of its resources and the growth of its population come into balance. Each man and woman—and each nation—must make decisions of conscience and policy in the face of this great problem."

"Freedom is not enough. You do not wipe away the scars of centuries. You do not take a man who for years has been hobbled by chains, liberate him, bring him to the starting line of a race saying, 'You are free to compete with all the others', and still justly believe you have been completely fair. Thus it is not enough to open the gates of opportunity."

"You know, doing what is right is easy. The problem is knowing what is right."

"Our society is illuminated by the spiritual insights of the Hebrew prophets. America and Israel have a common love of human freedom, and they have a common faith in a democratic way of life."

"You do not examine legislation in the light of the benefits it
will convey if property administration, but in the light
of the wrongs it would do and the harm it would cause if
improperly administered."

"Opinion and protest are the life breath of democracy – even when
it blows heavy."

"Books and ideas are the most effective weapons against intolerance
and ignorance."

37. RICHARD MILHOUS NIXON (1969-1974)

"When the President does it, that means that it is not illegal."

"This office is a sacred trust and I am determined to be worthy of
that trust."

"Government enterprise is the most inefficient and costly way of
producing jobs."

"Let us begin by committing ourselves to the truth—to see it like it
is, and tell it like it is—to find the truth, to speak the truth,
and to live the truth."

"I played by the rules of politics as I found them."

"This isn't going to be a good country for any of us to live in until
it's a good country for all of us to live in."

"There is no such thing as a nonpolitical speech by a politician."

"The word politics causes some people lots of trouble. Let us be
very clear = politics is not a dirty word."

"The people's right to change what does not work is one of the
greatest principles of our system of government."

"Any culture which can put a man on the Moon is capable of
gathering all the nations of the earth in peace, justice and
concord."

"America will not tolerate being pushed around by anybody, anyplace."

"No event in American history is more misunderstood than the Vietnam
War. It was misreported then, and it is misremembered, now."

"The greatest honor history can bestow is that of peacemaker."

"A public man must never forget that he loses his usefulness when he as an individual, rather than his policy, becomes an issue."

"Always remember, others may hate you. Those who hate you don't win unless you hate them. And then you destroy yourself."

"I don't think that a leader can control to any great extent his destiny. Very seldom can he step in and change the situation if the forces of history are running in another direction."

"The one thing sure about politics is that what goes up comes down and what goes down often comes up."

"The more you stay in this kind job, the more you realize that a public figure, major public figure, is a lonely man."

"Any change is resisted because bureaucrats have a vested interest in the chaos in which they exist."

"We seek friendly relations with all nations. Any nation can be our friend without being any other nation's enemy."

"The Cold War isn't thawing; it is burning with a deadly heat. Communism isn't sleeping; it is, as always, plotting, scheming, working, fighting."

"A man who has never lost himself in a cause bigger than himself has missed one of life's mountaintop experiences. Only in losing himself does he find himself."

"What kind of nation we will be, what kind of world we will live in, whether we shape the future in the image of our hopes, is ours to determine by our actions and our choices."

"I like the job I have, but if I had to live my life over again, I would like to have ended up a sports writer."

"Always give your best, never get discouraged, never be petty; always remember, others may hate you. Those who hate you don't win unless you hate them. And then you destroy yourself."

"I am not a crook."

"The finest steel has to go through the hottest fire."

"Castro wouldn't even go to the bathroom unless the Soviet Union put a nickel in the toilet."

"Defeat doesn't finish a man—quitting does. A man is not finished when he's defeated. He's finished when he quits."

"Finishing second in the Olympics, gets you silver. Finishing second in politics get you oblivion."

"It is time for the great silent majority of Americans to stand up and be counted."

"There is no such thing as a nonpolitical speech by a politician."

"Yet we can maintain a free society only if we recognize that in a free society no one can win all the time. No one can have his own way all the time, and no one is right all the time."

"The only way to achieve a practical, livable peace in a world of competing nations is to take the profit out of war."

"People react to fear, not love—they don't teach that in Sunday School, but it's true."

"Life isn't meant to be easy. It's hard to take being on the top— or on the bottom. I guess I'm something of a fatalist. You have to have a sense of history, I think, to survive of these things…Life is one crisis after another."

"I brought myself down. I impeached myself by resigning."

38. GERALD R. FORD (1974-1977)

"We … declared our independence 200 years ago, and we are not about to lose it now to paper shufflers and computers."

"The world is ever conscious of what Americans are doing, for better or for worse, because the United States today remains that most successful realization of humanity's universal hope. The world may ot may not follow, but we lead because whole industry says we must. Liberty is for all men and women as a matter of equal and unalienable right. The establishment of justice and peace abroad will in large measure depend upon the peace and justice we create here in our own country, and still show the way." (Bicentennial Remarks at Independence Hall, Philadelphia, PA, July 4, 1976)

"As we continue our American adventure…all our heroes and heroines of war and peace send us this single, urgent message: though prosperity is a good thing, though compassionate charity is a good thing, though institutional reform is a good thing, a nation survives only so long as the spirit of sacrifice and self-discipline is strong within its people. Independence has to be defended as well as declared; freedom is always worth fighting for; and liberty ultimately belongs only to those willing to suffer for it." (Bicentennial Remarks at Valley Forge, Pennsylvania, July 4, 1976)

"Remember, that none of us are more than caretakers of this great country. Remember, that the more freedom you give to others, the more you will have for yourself. Remember, that without law there can be no liberty. And remember, as the rich treasures you brought from whence you came, and let us share your price in them." (July 5, 1976)

"To me, the Presidency and the Vice-Presidency were not prizes to be won, but a job to be done." (Remarks upon accepting the Republican Nomination, Kansas, Missouri, August 19, 1976)

"We are bound together by the most powerful of all ties, our fervent love for freedom and independence, which knows no homeland, but the human heart! (Address before the Conference on Security and Cooperation in Europe – 8/1/1975)

"I am a Ford, not a Lincoln."

"I guess it just proves that in America anyone can be President."

"Indecision is often worse than wrong action." (Harvard Business Review, Sep/Oct 1987)

"He [Gerald R. Ford Sr.] and Mother had three rules: tell the truth, work hard, and come to dinner on time-and woe unto any of us who violated those rules." (From President Ford's memoir, A Time to Heal)

"Our Constitution works. Our great republic is a government of laws, not of men."

"The Constitution is the bedrock of all our freedoms, guard and cherish it; keep honor and order in your own house, and the republic will endure."

"Truth is the glue that holds governments together. Compromise is the oil that makes governments go." (Comment during U.S. House Committee hearing, 1973)

"In a democracy, the public has a right to know not only what the government decides, but why and by what process."

"A government big enough to give you everything you want is a government big enough to take from you everything you have."

"We needed to get the matter off my desk in the Oval Office, so I could concentrate on the problems of 260 million Americans and not have to worry about the problems of one man." (The pardoning of Richard Nixon)

"If Lincoln were alive today, he'd be turning over in his grave."

"The political lesson of Watergate is this: Never again must America allow an arrogant, elite guard of political adolescents to by-pass the regular party organization and dictate the terms of a national election."

"Richard Nixon was just offered $2 million by Schick to do a television commercial – for Gillette."

"My fellow Americans, our long national nightmare is over."

"I am acutely aware that you have not elected me as your president by your ballots, so I ask you to confirm me with your prayers."

"All of us who served in one war or another know very well that all wars are the glory and the agony of the young."

"When I became president, I did not want to have a powerful chief of staff. Wilson had the Colonel House, Eisenhower his Sherman Adams, Nixon had Halderman, and I was aware of the trouble those top assistants had caused my predecessors."

"When I talk about energy, I am talking about jobs. Our American economy runs on energy. No energy – no jobs."

"Most business leaders should do things that will convince the public that their interests go beyond making a buck." (Source: Harvard Business Review, Sep/Oct 1987)

"The American people want a dialogue between them and their President... And if we can't have that opportunity of talking with one another, seeing one another, shaking hands with one another, something has gone wrong in our society."

"To know John Kennedy, as I did, was to understand the true meaning of the word. He understood that courage is not something to be gauged in a poll or located in a focus group. No adviser can spin it. No historian can backdate it. For, in the age old contest between popularity and principle, only those willing to lose for their convictions are deserving of posterity's approval." (Accepting his John F. Kennedy Profiles in Courage Award)

"...The ultimate test of leadership is not the polls you take, but the risks you take. In the short run, some risks prove overwhelming. Political courage can be self-defeating. But the greatest defeat of all would be to live without courage, for that would hardly be living at all." (Accepting the John F. Kennedy Profile in Courage Award, May 21, 2001.)

"I watch a lot of baseball on the radio."

"I know I am getting better at golf because I am hitting fewer spectators."

"I don't think, if I had been president, on the basis of the facts as I saw them publicly. I don't think I would have ordered the Iraq was. I would have maximized our effort through sanctions, through restrictions, whatever, to find another answer. Rumsfeld and Cheney and the president made a big mistake in justifying going into the war in Iraq. They put the emphasis on weapons of mass destruction, and now, I've never publicly said I thought they made a mistake, but I felt very strongly it was an error in how they should justify what they were going to do." (Washington Post)

"I hope and trust that people and historians 50 years from now will write that the Ford administration took over in a very turbulent, controversial period, and we healed the wounds and that we restored the public trust in the White House and the presidency, I hope that's how it will be written."

39. JAMES E. CARTER JR. (1977-1981) LIVING

40. RONALD W. REAGAN (1981-1989)

"Within the covers of the Bible are all the answers for all he problems men face."

"America is too great for small dreams."

"Trust, but verify."

"A government bureau is the closest thing to eternal life we'll ever see on this earth."

"Government is like a baby. An alimentary canal with a big appetite at one end and no sense of responsibility at the other."

"Government is the people's business and every man, woman and child becomes a shareholder with the first penny of tax paid."

"Let us not forget who we are. Drug abuse is a repudiation of everything America is."

"Welfare's purpose should be to eliminate, as far as possible, the need for its own existence."

"But there are advantages of being elected President. The day after I was elected, I had my high school grades classified Top Secret."

"No matter what time it is, wake me, even if it's in the middle of a Cabinet meeting."

"A taxpayer is someone who works for the federal government but who doesn't have to take a civil service examination."

"We might come closer to balancing the Budget if all of us lived closer to the Commandments and the Golden Rule."

"Politics is supposed to be the second oldest profession. I have come to realize that it bears a very close resemblance to the first."

"Politics is just like show business, you have a hell of an opening, coast for a while and then have a hell of a close."

"We are a nation that has a government-not the other way around. And that makes us special among the nations of the earth."

"Mr. Gorbachev, tear down this wall."

"We cannot play innocents abroad in a world that is not innocent."

"The best minds are not in government. If any were, business would hire them away."

"Surround yourself with the best people you can find, delegate authority, and don't interfere."

"The government's view of the economy could be summed up in a few short phases: If it moves, tax it. If the beast keeps moving, regulate it. And if it stops moving, subsidize it."

"I believe that communism is another sad, bizarre chapter in human history whose last pages even now are being written."

"The more government takes in taxes, the less incentive people have to work."

"Government does not solve problems; its subsidizes them."

"No arsenal or no weapon in the arsenals of the world is so formidable as the will and moral courage of free men and women."

"Freedom prospers when religion is vibrant and the rule of law under God is acknowledged."

"The future does not belong to the faint-hearted. It belongs to the brave."

"No arsenal or no weapon in the arsenals of the world is so formidable as the will and moral courage of free men and women."

"Inflation is as violent as a mugger, as frightening as an armed robber and as deadly as a hit man."

"Government is not the solution to our problem, government is the problem."

"Evil is powerless if the good are unafraid."

"You can tell a lot about a fellow's character by his way of eating jelly beans."

"Information is the oxygen of the modern age. It seeps through the walls topped by barbed wires, it wafts across the electrified borders."

"Freedom is the recognition that no single person, no single authority or government has a monopoly on the truth, but that every individual life is infinitely precious, that every one of us put in this world has been put there for a reason and has something to offer."

"Freedom is the right to question and change the established way of doing things. It is the continuous revolution of the marketplace. It is the understanding that allows us to recognize shortcomings and seek solutions."

"I won a nickname. "The Great Communicator" But I never thought it was my style or the words I used that difference: It was the content. I wasn't the great communicator but I communicated great things, and they did spring full bloom from my brow, they came from the heart of a great nation—from our experience, our wisdom, and our belief in principles that have guided us for two centuries. They called it the Reagan revolution. Well, I'll accept that, but for me it always seemed more like the great rediscovery, a rediscovery of our values and our common sense."

"The lesson of all this was, of course, that because we're a great nation, our challenges seem complex. It will always be this way. But as long as we remember our first principles and believe in ourselves, the future will always be ours. And something else we learned: Once you begin a great movement, there's no telling were it will end. We meant to change a nation, and instead, we changed the world."

"Whatever else history may say about me when 'm gone, I hope it will record that I appealed to your best hopes, not your worst fears; to your confidence rather than your doubts. My dream is that you will travel the road ahead with liberty's lamp guiding your steps and opportunity's arm steadying your way.

"We've done our part. And as I walk of into the city streets, a final word to the men and women of the Reagan revolution, the men and women across America who for eight years did the work that brought America back. My friends: We did it, We weren't just marking time. We made a difference. We made the city stronger. We made the city freer, and we left her in good hands. Al in all, not bad, not bad at all. And so, goodbye, God bless you, and God bless the United States of America."

"I have recently been told that I am one of the millions of Americans who will be afflicted with Alzheimer's Disease...I now begin the journey that will lead me into the sunset of my life. I know that for America there will always be a bright dawn ahead."

41. GEORGE H. BUSH (1989-1993) LIVING

42. WILLIAM J. CLINTON (1993-2001) LIVING

43. GEORGE W. BUSH (2001- LIVING

ISBN 142512812-2